D0323324

"It is simply so good that I don't know how to praise it sufficiently.

"A brilliant analysis of the human condition, one of the very best I have ever seen. His earlier work (*The Crack in the Cosmic Egg*) was a penetrating analysis of how we are each trapped in a cosmic egg, a consensus reality, that severely limits our human potentials. Now he has elucidated the mechanisms of enculturation which alienate us from our natural wholeness, starting from our hidden fears of death and working up to the ways in which revolt and protest actually support the system. This is not a book for those who value their comforting illusions: it is must reading for those who realize the necessity of confronting the full horror of the prison we have made for ourselves as the necessary first step toward escape."

—Charles T. Tart, Ph.D.,
author of *Altered States of Consciousness*

EXPLORING THE CRACK IN THE COSMIC EGG
was originally published by The Julian Press.

Books by Joseph Chilton Pearce

The Crack in the Cosmic Egg
Exploring the Crack in the Cosmic Egg

Published by POCKET BOOKS

EXPLORING THE CRACK IN THE COSMIC EGG

Split Minds and Meta-realities

Joseph Chilton Pearce

PUBLISHED BY POCKET BOOKS NEW YORK

EXPLORING THE CRACK IN THE COSMIC EGG

Julian Press edition published 1974

POCKET BOOK edition published November, 1975

3rd printing........................June, 1976

This POCKET BOOK edition includes every word contained in the original, higher-priced edition. It is printed from brand-new plates made from completely reset, clear, easy-to-read type.

POCKET BOOK editions are published by
POCKET BOOKS,
a division of Simon & Schuster, Inc.,
A GULF+WESTERN COMPANY
630 Fifth Avenue,
New York, N.Y. 10020.
Trademarks registered in the United States
and other countries.

ISBN: 0-671-80638-6.

Library of Congress Catalog Card Number: 74-80124.

Front cover illustration by Michael Gross.

Printed in the U.S.A.

for Arthur Ceppos

Acknowledgments

To George Jaidar I owe my insight into fear as a learned reaction, and, though the elaborations are mine, I have borrowed from him the term "guilting" and the horse and rider analogy. Though my usage is quite different, I have borrowed "metaprogramming" from John Lilly's book, *Programming and Metaprogramming in the Human Biocomputer*.

My dedication, to my publisher, speaks for itself. Finally, my gratitude to Karen Hinds for her kindness and assistance, her red-pencil editing, proofreading, and stubborn refusal to let my obscurities pass unchallenged.

Contents

Introduction

In my book *The Crack in the Cosmic Egg,* I described reality as our semantic creation and explored how our minds could enter into that creation and change it. Accept the arbitrary nature of any reality representation, I argued, risk yourself to the transformation of it, and there are no limits to your creative capacity.

My experience since that writing has both verified *Crack* and yet forced certain revisions. For instance, what I called "autistic" thinking in *Crack* I now call "primary process thinking." The "reality-adjusted" thinking of *Crack* I now refer to as culturally conditioned thinking. These are not idle metaphoric exchanges, but radical shifts of viewpoint.

In *Crack*, I had failed to grasp certain fundamental principles because of unconsciously accepted cultural assumptions. I was fascinated by the interactions between mind and reality as displayed in *metanoia,* scientific discovery, spontaneous healings, fire-walking, and other nonordinary phenomena. But I found that "signs" and wonders did not alter our cultural plight in the least. And I found that while our "cosmic egg" is our own creation, not a "given state," that there *was* a "given state," a "primary process" lying untrammelled beyond the reach of our verbal warp. This I had denied previously.

I found, further, that we created a *Crack* for ourselves right along with our creation of our egg. That is, our biological development keeps our options open to the "given state" in spite of our cultural conditioning. Even as we seal ourselves into a word-built world, one function of our intellect breaks that seal and keeps our lines open. These "lines" lie not so much in our head as in what don Juan (see Carlos Castaneda's trilogy on the "teaching of don Juan") calls our "body-knowing." Again the evidence points toward two distinct modes of thinking, as it did in *Crack*.

Hans Furth (see bibliography) claims that the human intellect grows through living contact with the environment. This growth will take place *even where there is no linguistic system available*. Furth's observation runs counter to our acculturated beliefs, and surely challenges our educational bureaucracy. A child learns by interacting with reality in what I call our *Primary Program*. At the same time, however, the child must cope with the overwhelming impingement of cultural processing. I call this acculturation process our *Metaprogram*. This Metaprogram is an abstract semantic construct based not on reality interaction but on *fear* of reality. The child can only react to that fear with anxiety, and erect buffers to it, until he can intellectually create his *own* Metaprogram concepts. The ability for abstract conceptual creation opens somewhere around the sixth year of life. The child must devote his new capacity to structuring the cultural "semantic reality" *in order to survive that reality system*. As a result, his Primary Program, biologically endowed, is overlaid and dominated by a cultural "reality adjustment." The process is largely completed by adolescence.

Certain biological shifts nevertheless take place to offset this acculturation procedure. By these shifts, our

Primary Program continues development. The organism succeeds in retaining its original biological intent, though it must use "nonsemantic" modalities for that end. The existence of this "body-knowing," apparently below our awareness, is one of the issues of this book.

While my exploration involves "nonordinary" phenomena, I use such material with reservations. The area of "paranormal" phenomena suffers as seriously from the misappropriations of its enthusiasts as from the scoffings of the academicians. So-called "psychic" phenomena is a natural expression of our logical possibilities, a biological "norm" masked by acculturation. I question the validity of such terms as "extrasensory perception," and doubt the validity of using scientific models for the mystery of mind's interaction with reality.

To explore your own Crack, you must first find that Crack. To find the Crack, some understanding of our egg and the texture of shells will help. So in the first half of this work I will explore the "egg" itself—"how" this "spectacular misunderstanding" occurs. The second half will then explore some aspects of the Crack, as far as words can convey this sort of thing.

No "hidden powers of the mind" are to be uncovered here. My aim is to bankrupt your semantic hope chests, and empty the coffers of your pipe dreams so readily provided by culture.

As Joel Latner says, "to be aware, we must have empty heads." He then relates my favorite Zen story of Nan-in, a nineteenth century Japanese Master, who received a university professor coming to inquire about Zen. As Nan-in silently prepared tea, the professor expounded at length on his own philosophies and insights. Nan-in quietly filled his visitor's cup *and then kept right on pouring.* Alarmed at the tea spilling all over, ruining the immaculate ceremony, the professor exclaimed: "It is full, no more will go in."

"Like this cup," Nan-in said, "you are already full of your own opinions and speculations. How can I show you Zen unless you first empty your cup?"

So my invitation in the following pages is for you to examine your cup, to discover just how full it already is, and to examine the nature of its contents. Only when we are willing to accept the nature of our cups and contents are we willing to accept emptiness.

Should anyone tell you what happens when your cup empties, they are telling you a tale. Listen if you like—storytelling is fun. But what happens to the empty cup lies beyond all our conjectures, and outside all our speech.

Part One

Prelude

Our experience is our reality. We are social creatures by nature, and sharing our experience has established a *consensus,* or common agreement, *about* reality. We accept this consensus as our *culture,* that is, the matrix from which our experience is derived. While our consensus *functions* culturally, the results are destructive. For our agreement acts as an artificial overlay, a semantic screen, blinding us to a process, a *given* matrix, this is truly "cultural."

We are conditioned from birth to accept the overlay as vital to survival, though it fails us in every way, and to react to the flow of our natural matrix as tantamount to death. This contradiction shapes our perceptions of the world, society, and our self. It literally *splits* our minds and makes of us our own adversary.

I know of no way to explore this contradiction other than treating this overlay as our *antagonist.* The technique is an old one. To perceive the real instead of the illusory, don Juan, the Yaqui "Man of Knowledge," insists that his apprentice confront and accept his own death, a notion in contradiction to consensus conditioning.

This "giving up of life in order to find life" is certain to be sensed as an ultimate threat. Paradoxical on the surface, I hope to show the biological function beneath the covering of words. The issue is truly, as don Juan said, a matter of "body-knowing."

1. Stable Sameness

Carlos Castaneda saw some young Mexican bootblacks eating the scraps off plates at a sidewalk café. He felt sorry for them, deprived as they were of education, opportunities, and cultural advantages. Don Juan was contemptuous of Carlos' sentiment, however, and pointed out that any of those boys could become a Man of Knowledge. He further implied that they could do so with greater ease than Carlos, since their heads wouldn't be filled with as much nonsense.

In my book *The Crack in the Cosmic Egg,* I examined the way our thinking enters into the structuring of our reality. I showed how transformation of our concepts about reality could change aspects *of* our reality. My contention, that "man's mind mirrors a universe that mirrors man's mind," ran counter to the accepted world view. Extreme as my claims were, though, they were only suggestive of the radical break implied by don Juan in his reply to Carlos.

In *Crack,* I wrote of an arbitrary nature to our "semantic universe," but I considered this just the arbitrary nature of our reality. I didn't realize that a "semantic reality" was a cultural artifice. I thought it our "given," or natural process. I accepted the necessity of such an artifice without question. Above all, it never occurred to me that *culture* as a necessary prerogative could itself be the real issue. For culture is so "axiomatic" that our minds respond to it just as our bodies respond to gravity. The most formative influences of our lives are beyond awareness and simply "happen to us."

A statement from Whitehead, used in *Crack,* is needed again, here: "There will be some fundamental assumptions which adherents of all the variant systems within the epoch unconsciously presuppose. Such assumptions appear so obvious that people do not know what they are assuming because no other way of putting things has ever occurred to them."[1]

There is a creative and joyful anarchy inherent within don Juan's reply to Carlos, but we can't "hear it" because of fundamental cultural assumptions shaping our hearing itself. For who would question that culture represents the highest achievement of life? Or that civilization as practiced by us is not the "great goal of evolution"? We have been conditioned to believe this implicitly. We presume that without culture man would be only another animal, a creature of darkness without meaning or purpose.

To assert, then, that culture is *not* a necessary prerogative, nor indeed even the proper vehicle for man's venture, seems preposterous. It seems more ridiculous to claim that language is more a tragedy than a blessing precisely because it does just what the academics reiterate: "gives to us our enormous heritage of acquired experience and knowledge." Every war demonstrates anew that we never learn from such "acquired experience," or benefit from such "inherited knowledge." Nor does sending men into space, and plunging ever deeper into a technological morass, assuage our inner despair.

Leslie White spoke of culture as an "organism" with

life and death cycles of its own. But the cultural effect, by which we are conditioned, blinds us to a *primary process* that is our true source of communion and social being. Each of us is born with a "life scheme" that is masked, inhibited, and finally dominated by the process of acculturation. For all intents and purposes, this *primary program,* that is our birthright, becomes nonexistent through acculturation. Once our *primary program* is masked into noncognizance, culture emerges as the dominant *meta program* in our organism.

Once this *meta program* of culture becomes dominant, it shapes our experience into an arbitrary and parallel *counterfeit* of that which is real. Once this *meta program* takes over our perceptual apparatus, it is the only mode we then have for interacting with reality. Once that happens we can't question our culturally conditioned state, since that is our only reality experience.

Our mental-physical organism unfolds from its germ as a leaf from its bud, without assistance from a word-built intellect. But this "natural program" is overlaid by the cultural one. The cultural meta program parallels, imitates, and intertwines with our natural process. Gradually it becomes the dominant force in our biological system.

Back in the 1940's, Harry Stack Sullivan made the following comment, which is apropos to don Juan's contempt of Carlos's sentiment, and germane to this book:

"The origin of the self-system [our ego-awareness, JP] can be said to rest on the irrational character of culture. Were it not for the fact that a great many prescribed ways of doing things have to be lived up to, in order that one shall maintain . . . relations, or, were the prescriptions for the types of behavior in carrying on relations with one's fellows perfectly *rational* [my italics, JP], then, for all I know, there would not be evolved, in the course of becoming a person, anything like the sort of self-system that we always encounter."[2]

In don Juan, Jesus, certain Zen and Sufi figures, we get a glimpse of what might be possible for a "self-system" not dominated by acculturation, and a reality not shaped by the cultural semantic. We then see most of the problems attributed to "human nature" as artificial results from acculturation.

Culture operates by "taking over" some, and heavily influencing other, biological functions in each of us. Equally, however, culture is the result of certain biological functions in "conflict" with other biological functions. For instance, we possess "new brain" processes that are essentially discontinuous with older brain functions. They are capable of operations for which none of our older brain systems seem "preparatory" in any way. Our newer brain processes are designed for symbolic representations, abstractions, creative logic, speech, and other aspects of "operational thinking," as Piaget calls it. Our older brain systems, on the other hand, are more involved with "homeostasis," survival, and well being. These older autonomous systems work to keep a stable relationship between the various parts of our body and our "ambient," or life-sphere as a whole.

A tension between these diverse and apparently unrelated mental functions is inevitable. Culture is the end result of our outward "projection" of this internal dominance-conflict.[3] The cultural effect results from an "intellectual warping" of our survival system, on the one hand, and from our survival system "crippling" our intellect, on the other. And which effect "comes first" is a chicken-egg kind of riddle.

Thinking is an act, a process. To *think* is to react to, respond to, or interact with, reality. Much reality interaction takes place that is nonverbal and even "noncerebral." We are consciously "aware" of only certain end products of thinking, even though thinking is an all-inclusive act. Any aspect of thinking tends to incorporate all other aspects of thinking. *Homeostasis,* for instance, (a survival process to be discussed shortly), is as active a part of thinking as talking, but takes place largely outside our ego-awareness.

Our thinking apparatus is elaborate and mysterious. It involves our entire body and encompasses even more than just our organism. Charles Tart, of the University of California at Davis, relates an experiment in which a subject sat in a soundproofed room designed for sensory-deprivation studies. The subject was "wired up" for brain wave recordings, skin resistance, heart rate, muscular activity, respiratory changes, and so on, all recorded on a "polygraph" machine. Down the hall, in a similar chamber, an "agent" or sender was electrically shocked at random intervals. The subject was asked to guess *when* the sender was being shocked. The subject's polygraph reading indicated significant physiological changes at those instants when the agent was randomly shocked. But the subject's *conscious guesses* at when the shocks occurred showed no relation to the actual events as related by his polygraph readings.[4]

We say the event did not register on the subject's "conscious mind." But obviously he *was* conscious of the event—on a fundamental, biological level. The subject's *body* apparently knew of these happenings that his "roof-brain" or ego-awareness did not know about. Tart's experiment gives us a glimpse into what don Juan meant by "body-knowing." Two mental modes of function are involved, as I outlined in my book, *Crack*.

Tart's example indicates a kind of "knowing" connected with our environ, or life envelope. The way Tart designed his experiment determined the nature of the subject's temporary "environ," and determined the kind of data selected from the "flow" *of* that environ. In the same way, our *primary program* selects from the "flow" around it those aspects vital to our individual organism. But, just as Tart's subject had no ego-awareness of his body-knowing's response, so, as acculturated people, we suffer a "communication gap" between these fundamental modes of our mind. This gap leaves us feeling alienated from our life process, an isolation and despair that all the technologies of our creation cannot assuage.

Our newer brain functions give unique capacities for reflective thinking and creative logic, functions offering an infinitely open possibility. But, because of our split of self, we suffer a "failure of nerve" when our creative thinking starts to move us beyond our known stable sameness carried autonomously within our older brain-body systems. These biological survival drives are too well ingrained for transformation. Yet the strength of our newer, intellectual-creative processes will not be denied completely. And culture's "semantic reality" is the creative stasis resulting from these thinking dynamisms in conflict.

In the following chapters I will show how culture forces each of us to create this "pseudoreality" structured around the semantic effect of language, and how culture "substitutes" a semantic reality for a direct reality interaction. Culture's word-built world acts as a stimulus substitute that replaces, changes, curtails, or mutates stimuli from a real world. What we experience as acculturated people is never the free interaction with our life flow, that for which we are designed by our "primary programming." Rather, we experience a life flow filtered through an ideation scheme sharply altering our real world.

Culture arises from and rests squarely on what I call a "death concept." This is a notion resulting from reflections on death, and a belief in a universal "hostility" toward life. This intellectually conceived notion confuses and disorients the intellectual and survival drives, the two apparently "opposed" modes of mind. The "semantic reality" results, an ideation scheme that serves as an *intermediary between* our senses and our percepts.[5] This mediant effect interprets as a "buffer" between self and hostile world. Since the semantic mediant is an imaginary creation, we can imaginatively change it within our heads. This gives us the illusion of prediction and control over our environment. This maneuver interprets as successful death-avoidance.

The assumption that the universe is hostile to life is never clearly formulated. In fact, it would be denied by most of us, even with embarrassment. Yet this notion is manifested on every hand, by implication and inference. The assumption induces a cast of thinking in each of us that actually produces results accordingly. A kind of mass cultural projection mirrors this "judgment against life," which is then seen outwardly as the universe's "judgment" against us.

Culture as a paradigm of life couldn't take place without the anxiety effect of this "death concept."

The anxiety effect of this notion is a large part of the fabric of our life sphere, and is induced into each of us from infancy. The death concept becomes the principal influence in our interaction with reality. The concept mediates between our sense and percept, and a hostile universe is actually perceived to be the case.

For *perceptions* are end products of our thinking, final results of our mind's acting on reality data.[6] Our senses are exposed to and respond to vast amounts of reality data of which we are never "consciously aware." An enormous amount of varied sensory activity goes on in the body at all times—and only selected items are processed as "perceived events."

Our intellect acts on reality data through patterns called "concepts." Concepts are rather "imprintings" by which we connect reality data into units for cognition, or awareness. Certain biological processes shape data according to our *primary program,* as suggested in Tart's experiment cited earlier. Other processes shape data according to the semantic reality induced through acculturation—as witnessed by our ordinary, fear-filled, anxiety-ridden, consensus reality. Based on the assumption of a hostile universe, the semantic reality, acting as mediant between sense and percept, breeds a hostile reality. Our primary program, functioning always for unity or wholeness, is thus working in opposition to the semantic process. This gives some indication of our split within.

Since the reality out-there appears hostile to our conditioned minds—filtering that reality through the death concept, as we do—culture seems the proper medium for growth, our source of nourishment, our protective umbrella against the cosmic fallout, and our only "hope." Nature is the grim adversary, while culture becomes the "surrogate mother," a buffer standing between our frail lives and the blind uncaring universe.

This judgment against life is never stated so baldly. It is always cloaked as something else, and couched with common-sense, rational observations. That such common sense always leads to chaos and discord is accepted as our "natural condition." This is a breakdown of biological functioning. There is no need for *ad hoc* principles of a religious or philosophical nature to explain this "fall of man." Studying the development of intellect in infants and children is more productive.

It was long held axiomatic, for instance, that conceptual thinking, and "abstract, logical thought," were products of language. Without language we should be both dumb as beasts and incapable of logical action.

This seemed so self-evident that few questioned it seriously. Yet Jean Piaget and Hans Furth were led to question just this "axiomatic" position, and from different pursuits. Piaget studied the growth of intelligence in infants from their birth, before either language or logical development had begun. He followed their development through childhood, as logical ability unfolded. Hans Furth devoted ten years to a study of thinking in congenitally deaf children who had no linguistic ability at all.

Their work dovetailed. Each reinforced their common conclusions: that the infant begins logical thinking before he learns a language; that symbolic creation comes before word-thinking; and that the highest forms of "operational thinking" can, and often should, take place outside language entirely.[7]

In *Crack* I had placed logical thinking in opposition to "autistic" or what I now call *Primary Process* thinking. In this I was partially mistaken. The split of mind created by acculturation doesn't follow any neat party lines (as suggested by recent "split-brain" research, for instance) but affects every aspect of our mentality.

Furth and Piaget, in giving us tools for examining conceptual and logical growth, have given us tools for examining the growth of culture. For culture *is* our set of concepts by which we interact with reality. Interacting through our cultural sets *creates* our cultural reality. Process and product are the same. We each, individually, create our own cultural concepts in keeping with our culture *in order to survive our culture.* Then, because these conceptual creations are our own, biological responses, they are "below awareness," the only way by which our consciousness can operate. The reality resulting is then not only ultimately valuable as our very life, but beyond the possibility for questioning. To think outside this mode of thinking is equivalent to lifting one's self by one's bootstraps.[8]

Concept is loosely used, and I need to clarify my use of it. Conceptual thinking can be considered an "internalized form of sensory-motor action." Just as a child will fit building blocks together according to some "plan" of physical movement, so the *concept* is an internalized plan by which intellect acts on the "building blocks" of reality data.[9] For we can act on data only according to some schematic. Conceptual thinking is a "transactive movement" by which our intellect puts together those reality components we entertain or respond to.

None of our senses "stand alone." All must "cross-index," in what is called synesthesia, to be shaped into a perceived event. The child blind from birth and given sight through an operation "sees" only a sea of color blotches. These blotches must undergo conceptual structuring, modification by all the other senses, to finally emerge as "cognizable" shapes. Cognition must fit the new sense into the criteria developed from birth, a combination of sound, taste, smell, touch, and perhaps other subtle sensings. Older persons given sight through an operation find the new visual stimuli intensely disorienting. They must close their eyes to reestablish their identity with reality. The newly seeing child still identifies the tree by feel, smell, touch, and even taste. It is only then that she notices "the tree has lights in it."

Our conceptual patterns form from birth, but the process of acculturation can't "induce" such patterns into the mind. Rather, our concepts are our personal, biological creations. From our beginnings we created such patterns as our response, or "reality adjustment," to the world. We interacted with the real world in our first six years or so through transactive movements of *primary processing*. Culture, however, is a set of imaginative expectancies. To interact with the world of our culture we had to create the necessary concepts. Cultural concepts are abstract creations. Abstract logic and creation is a later development of intellectual growth, unfolding somewhere after our sixth year.

To be acculturated, then, is not to be handed a specific set of concrete ideas concerning reality. Each of us creates culture anew. The demand that we make this creative response comes about in many ways, predominantly through fear. The flexibility and tenaciousness of the cultural effect lies in its lack of clarity. (Subtle doubt can create far more havoc than dogmatic condemnation.)

The building of concepts is a total biological process, not just a "head-trip." Conceptual thinking is a *homeostatic function.* The word *homeostatis* means "stable sameness," the title of this chapter. *Homeostasis* is a term given our biological functions building and maintaining a stable worldview. Our "flight-fight syndrome," for instance, is a warning device that "rings the bell" of alarm when our stability is threatened. *Homeostasis* means what the system does —organizes our body senses to keep a stable identity for our awareness.

"Stable sameness" operates on three interlocking levels: 1) communication between the myriad cells and organs of our body; 2) our overall cognitive system perceiving reality as whole events; 3) our relationship between our cognizing organism and our ambient, or life envelope in which we live.

In our strange, dissective cultural view, we have recognized only the interrelating that maintains a stable relation in the body as our "homeostatic system." By and large we have ignored, by selective inattention, our equally important symbiotic relation with our environment and the "life-flow system" as a whole. At best such a function is suggested only in esoteric ways that fragment it. We speak of "altered states of consciousness," telepathy, clairvoyance, and so on, to refer to the fragmented bits of the function breaking through our fixed notions. In the example of Charles Tart's work, we were given a glimpse of the subtle ways we relate with a "life flow," and I hope to clarify the process further.

Our biological functions of homeostasis and "flight-fight" are incorporated into and trained to respond to cultural concepts. Equally, however, these functions both give rise to, and provide a basis for, our cultural response. Our selective blindness concerning our symbiotic relations with the life flow is itself a product of acculturation. Culture views our life system as a potential hostility, and trusts only that which we intellectually construct and manipulate. This means that we learn to trust and use only certain limited acts of mind, and inhibit all other mental modalities. The mirroring effect between our thinking and our reality then gives us a reality isolated from our life-flow system. Our concepts shape our percepts and we "see" accordingly.[10]

Here are four widely varying examples of "homeostasis." The first example is taken from an experiment in cognition-studies. The second example is (to be kind) psychosocial by nature, an example of keeping one's social image of self stabilized. The third example is rather a combination of the first two. The fourth example is taken from animal life and shows how homeostasis relates with the life-flow system, and how the "flight-fight system" is any disruption of homeostasis.

In studies of perception, subjects were fitted with goggles that turned their visual image upside down. The goggles were worn constantly, the subjects having to adjust to an upside-down world as best they could. After several days, however, the visual process suddenly *righted* that upside-down vision of the world. After a time the goggles were removed. And immediately the world was seen *upside down* again. After about the same period of adjustment time, however, the inordinately complex relationship between eye-brain-mind again reversed the reversal, and turned that world viewed back upright.

This is the clearest example of our biological function called homeostasis. Keeping intact our known world-identity or "stable sameness" is a survival function that our body carries on without any help from our ego "roof-brain" activity.

Thinking in any form is always related to such an internal, organized structure. The goggle-subject's ego-awareness had nothing specific to do with these visual reversals. Rather, ego-thinking plays on the surface of a rich backdrop of stable conceptual patterns. These patterns function below awareness and are locked into the very fibre of our body.

Once one's world view has formed in this way, it does not lend itself easily to change. And the world view formed contains far more than a simple orientation to up and down. Our ego-thinking can rearrange some of the given fixtures on the surface, and even create novel effects, but we can do little to alter the conceptual framework built from infancy.

Again, I was giving a talk for one of those week-end seminars. Afterward, as I was having lunch, a dear little lady sat down to express her appreciation of my talk. She had understood me so clearly, she reported, because her Spiritual Guide, Brother Lawrence (*The Practice of the Presence of God* Brother Lawrence, mind you) had been right there in her right ear translating and explaining everything to her.

The dear little lady proceeded to relate to me Brother Lawrence's interpretation, which lasted about the same hour's time as my talk. At any rate, from beginning to end I could not find one toehold of recognition in her discourse. Off we went into astrology, spiritualism, reincarnation, astral projection, Madam

Blavatsky, dream interpretation, Edgar Cayce, you name it. All of which was *my* talk—the one *I* thought had been on perception, cognition, and so on.

(I knew then it made little difference what one said in a speech, as it may not make much difference what one writes. Listeners hear as they need to hear.)

The little lady's homeostatic drive served her criteria system of social-self. "Brother Lawrence" was her mediating device by which she acted on her "incoming data," converting it as needed for service to her world view. Her prism of prejudice acted on her data just as effectively as the image-goggles in the visual experiment.

Through acculturation, there is little difference in function between "biological" and psychosocial. Each supports the other to maintain the self-system. Only in early childhood might our sensory-perceptual system move as a unified, unbroken act.

From studies in cognition again: subjects were placed before a screen and shown a picture out of focus. The subjects were asked to study the blurred image until they could begin to perceive the original form. After sufficient time, the subjects did, indeed, begin to "see" what was there.

Once the visual image "formed" for them and their strained sensory-perceptual system relaxed with its created image, the experimentor would then bring the blur into focus. The actual picture never related to the imagined constructs and the point was for the experimentor to time the subjects' adaptations to the picture as it actually was. An average of forty-five seconds elapsed before the subjects became aware that the picture had "changed." (Try forty-five seconds and you will find it to be quite a while.)

Even more intriguing was a variation of this experiment. When the subject finally began to "see" what the blur was, the experimentor, without changing the blur, challenged the *rightness* of the subject's construction. This threatened the self-system's hard-won orientation. The more the subject's "seeing" was challenged, the more tenacious and firm his "seeing" became.

On bringing the image into clear focus, these subjects took—not forty-five seconds to shift and adapt—but up to three minutes for their visual process to perceive the new sensory data. (You might remember this in your next heated argument.)

Here are some of the aspects of homeostasis. If only a "blur" is offered, and the demand is made for accommodation to, and identification of, that blur, the cognitive system transacts according to the pattern of one's background. We fit that which is unknown into our known reference scheme, both as a way of clarifying the reality in which we move, and of keeping our known background stable.

Do not underestimate this power for keeping the world intact and familiar. That it operates largely below awareness is its strength. That it incorporates our social self is its subtlety. Further, *suggestiveness,* which needs our subjective clarification, as found in the blurred image experiment, is one of the most effective of all influences. Through such suggestive demands for response we create our reaction, so to speak. Since we are then reacting to our own creation, we are doubly convinced of the validity of our response.

All of us have a Brother Lawrence in our right ear, interpreting and explaining; just as we all wear goggles inverting the image of reality, whether we are aware of it or not. The blurred images resulting must be given shape and then defended by our rationale, for our survival system is at stake.

Our goggles and Brother Lawrences in the ear are culture. This metaprogram shapes every aspect of our lives. It is a force that we are so conditioned by that we are not aware of its action. No other way of being seems conceivable, nor is any other way of transacting with reality ordinarily employed within our experience.

Once built into the organism, this process of culture will not be rooted out. Yet the notion that it can be rooted out, that it can be "corrected" and put in proper order, is also a part of our cultural conditioning and vital to cultural preservation.

For my final example here of homeostasis, consider Rabbit—not rabbit-in-the-wilds, but very Urbane Rabbit. I watched him for weeks one semester of graduate school. We shared a secluded, sunny little flower garden each afternoon. Surrounded by high, thick hedges, our little island world was private but very noisy—for it was situated at a crowded, busy, intersection, filled with car honkings, squeals, slammings, and the incessant chatter and clatter of pedestrians on the sidewalk.

Since I kept very still, Rabbit ignored me completely. He also ignored the traffic noise, which I found an abrasive intrusion. No flicker of recognition reaction ever came from Rabbit over any of the background din, only feet away from us. Even the big, unexpected, crisis noises brought no reaction from those long ears, calmly lying in repose as he ate flower blossoms at leisure.

All I had to do, however, was scratch on the lawn with my fingers, no matter where in the garden Rabbit was, and instantly those long ears flicked to attention and he froze to alert. I repeated this many times and was intrigued that while I could never hear the scratchings myself, (the decibel overlay of traffic was considerable), Rabbit heard though twenty feet away.

Rabbit's homeostatic system had long since identified all the forms of traffic noises and cataloged them as needing no further attention. The scratching in the grass, though, was not of the known and familiar. This sensory item was admitted to his cognitive system and relayed on into that final act we call a percept. Rabbit filtered out the powerful but extraneous and attended only the subtle though meaningful. His performance indicates the nature of our life-flow connection lost to us through acculturation, and the nature of the "threat-syndrome" act resulting from this larger frame of reference.

There is a strange reversal of Rabbit's order of things in our acculturated system. We use the reversal for certain transactions, but an equal function and possibility needed by us is filtered out and lost thereby.

Let me outline this loss briefly, though prematurely, and return to it later. Our sensory-perception system is trained to attend the noisy background, while a scratching-in-the-grass kind of signal is screened out. The subtle signals are screened out both by selective inattention training, and sheer decibel drowning-out from that background we are trained to attend.

Rabbit's homeostatic set of stable familiarity acts as a *mediant* between his sense and percept, in that it stops the useless at that point. Acculturation assures us that *our* sensory perceptual system will lock in on that source of traffic, so to speak, since that *is* culture. To be acculturated is to lock out the natural world and attune the thinking apparatus to cultural products. The social-semantic then acts as the mediant between our sense and percept in a way opposite to Rabbit's. We are then "reality adjusted" to the semantic reality, not to the world as itself. The mediant effect works equally on our interaction with people as well as things of the world. Once acculturated, we act on data with our conceptual sets, rather than interacting with data in creative ways.

I am in no way suggesting a "back-to-nature" romantic revolt. The "nature" to which I refer is our natural, given state of communion, which is as operative and effective in the heart of a metropolis as in don Juan's desert or Jesus's Galilee.

Later I will outline how homeostasis enters into language development and how language development then influences the homeostatic system. This interplay is the way our organism is shifted from reality orientation to a semantic orientation, so that semantic feedback becomes the issue of "flight-fight" survival maneuvers, and word data substitutes for reality data as the mind's material for interaction.

Homeostasis is such a commonplace effect that it is unnoticeable. We overlook the extensive and continual adjustments we make as stability-seeking creatures. It isn't so much that we "have" a homeostatic system as that we behave "homeostatically" on very fundamental levels.

Paradoxically, through acculturation we seek stability by trying to change things according to semantic conceptions. In this way we maintain a "semantic reality" supposedly amenable to our homeostatic drive. This creation of a metareality is a misuse of a logical capacity, and fragments our possibilities afforded by logic as a cocreative effect in reality. The first half of this book explores the formation of culture as a circular effect between homeostasis and creativity. For culture is itself an expression of the homeostatic drive in conflict with creative thinking. At the same time, culture is *itself* creative thinking, oriented to, warped by, and in service of, this fundamental biological process.

We think of culture "fostering" creative thinking, as found in art and science. Consider instead that creativity is moving from the known to the unknown and always must emerge in spite of culture. Culture immediately warps any creative product to some extent, changes its thrust, and utilizes it for culture. Were it not for creativity, culture itself would not be created.

In order to show the cultural effect I will briefly outline the growth of logical and creative thinking in the child. This will entail outlining the parallel effect of the use of mediation in thinking. Then it will be more clear why the homeostatic-cultural effect moves to block our creative capacity and orient us to semantic channels through the use of mediation in thinking.

Mediation is one of the great logical tools available to mind. Through it we can create reality spheres for adventurous interaction. Through mediation we can "mutate the metaphors" by which we represent a reality situation, and so change that situation. Through acculturation, however, mediation becomes a buffering device, or an insulator, designed to shield us from a "hostile universe." That this buffer effect succeeds only in isolating us from the life flow and so creates the "human condition" of anxiety, fear, and alienation, is just a bad joke we bring on ourselves.

My intent is not to "condemn" culture, (condemning gravity for a skinned knee would be more fruitful), nor is my intent to suggest "correctives" for the cultural process. We stagger under a landslide of such suggestions continually. I do hope to suggest that no aspect of culture is in any way correctable, and I further hope to show that negative attention strengthens culture as fully as positive. And just to round it out, I hope to show that you can't ignore culture and survive it.

The protest, the antiwar rally, the sit-in, the moral outrage, the mass-righteous indignations, the countercultural enthusiasms, act as vital escape valves for the cultural process. Excess frustration boils off thereby, in order that the culture might continue unhindered doing just as it is going to do. (The great apathy following the Vietnam protest movement was intuitive recognition of this fated fact.)

Culture and its "civilization" is don Juan's World of Folly; the world of illusion in Indian metaphysics; and Jesus's Mammon World, *in* which we apparently *must* be, but *of* which we do not *have* to be.

To ask "what then" is proposed for man's world is pointless, for that world *is* culture, always has been, and always will be. As to what the world might be through orientation to a Jesus or a don Juan, such questions could only be answered by being that process itself, a process in which these kinds of culturally motivated questions would not arise.

Man's history has been the continual attempt to deal with the irrational aspects of his cultural function. So I will explore this function in the hopes of showing the futility of trying to "escape" it or change it. My concern will be to strip away hope, the cultural "ace-up-the-sleeve" seduction game. For only at a point of genuine bankruptcy of hope can we glimpse beyond our cultural conditioning and sense a possible turning.

Our acculturation conditions us to *do:* to strive for, earn, compete, win, seize, scheme, design, ensnare overcome, make-up, mock-up, structure-up, invent, and kill for if need be. This is *doing*. This is the modern cultural desire to change things. (Don Juan tells Carlos: you can change nothing.)

A secondary concern of this work will be the raft of *meta-metaprograms* clamoring to be a way, or the way, out of the cultural bind. Culture *is* the *meta-program.* No variation of the cultural metaprogram can simulate the Primary Program, nor can any combination of the metaprogram remove that meta-program. The cultural process is self-replicating, designed to reproduce its own process-product circularity.

Every action from our culturally conditioned thinking only enhances the cultural position. And through acculturation, we are left with no other way of thinking. Each variation of metaprogramming may afford novelty, entertainment, and temporary relief from despair, but all of this is simply a shift of mediation device. The stakes are far higher.

We can't, by taking thought–or *doing* in the cultural sense–increase our stature by a cubit. The acorn doesn't become an oak by such "doing." It is simply programmed to become an oak–as we are programmed to become fully human. Unfortunately we are also metaprogrammed. This word-built conceputal scheme parallels and imitates the development of the Primary one, and finally wins out as the system of dominance in our organism.

The only way around the dominance of the metaprogram is *not-doing* in the don Juan or Eugen Herrigel "Zen-sense." Doing *is* the metaprogram. So long as we think we can change things, we are holding to "doing." Even "changing ourselves" is generally only another variant of doing, a meta-metaprogram number. There is nothing we can do to return to the initial, or Primary Program any more than a leaf could return to its bud.

"Not-doing" opens our percepts to that which has unfolded within us right along, in spite of the metaprogram.

Hints of the Primary Process abound, as exemplified by don Juan, Zen, Jesus, bits from the Sufi, Buddhism, and the Tao. Each is covered with nonsense sooner or later, and even the glimpses afford us, at best, only second-hand access. They are signs only, and to grasp a sign (doing) is to lose its signification.

2. Sensory-Mediant Perception

Building the Semantic Universe

Culture and language grow out of each other in chicken-egg fashion. Learning to talk is the cultural equivalent of learning to walk in gravity. For culture rests on the semantic effect and the possiblities for mediation that language holds.

Cultural concepts, too, can act as "intermediaries" between sense and percept. For, as pointed out, a concept functions as a verb, not a noun. A concept arcs the gaps between the varied data contributed by all our senses, and welds them into units perceived as reality.[1] Our whole organism is involved in creating our concepts in the first place.[2] After that, *supporting* our conceptual sets is equivalent to survival itself.

Abstract concepts, having no basis in immediate reality, can alter our interacting with real things, and so change the nature of our reality experience. Fear, for instance, may be "only imagination," and yet influence the way we interact with our world.

Anxiety, as "fear without an object," can influence conceptual patterns, and alter our experience of real things.

Moving from the known to the unknown is the way of intellectual growth and creativity, the way we explore reality and learn new things. But the side effects of anxiety and fear can impede movements from the known to the unknown, and block creative explorations into reality.

Tracing the infant's reality exploration, and his resulting intellectual growth, throws light on the way culture is created, and the way anxiety both influences and grows out of such a creation.

One of the instinctive movements an infant is born with, for instance, is the sucking response to "nipple in the mouth." Yet the infant will actually *reject* the nipple offered by a severely anxiety-ridden mother, even though his survival depends on nursing.[3] And just as he will reject an "anxiety-ridden nipple" in the beginning, the child will later try to reject an anxiety-ridden reality by turning to semantic mediation as a buffer to his fear.

In a sense, all infant thinking is "creative." Such creativity must start from a given, or "known," base, however, and we are, indeed, born with just such a base. Recent studies have determined that the newborn *does* focus his eyes and see soon after birth, contrary to previous assumptions. But he sees very selectively, apparently being born with the ability to cognize only a *human face*. Photographic studies show that the newborn will pick out from a variety of possible visual targets that one that most resembles a human face, if an actual face is not present. The infant will devote 80 percent of his "visual time" in fixed focus on that face. If the visual targets are moved around, the infant's focus shifts accordingly, zeroing in again on that face.

This face cognition gives the infant his stable reference point for visual exploration. *Intellectual growth starts* when the baby starts shifting his focus from the "mothering-one's" face, his "known," to other objects, the "unknown."[4] This is the beginning of concept construction and identity. Following the lead of visual exploration, the infant physically grasps for objects sighted. Grasped, he then *tastes* the object, if he can, for identification, since tasting is the tactile sense most developed at this stage.

The infant builds a context of known things through such concrete experience. Remove an object toward which he grasps at this stage, however, and his attention will shift to another tangible object. Shift an object grasped for *behind* another object, easily within grasp but out of visual line, and the infant's attention still shifts immediately to another item. An object removed from immediate sight is a nonexistent object during these early months.

A dramatic change in this pattern occurs a little before the first year. The infant will suddenly begin to *search* for that object when it is removed. Piaget claims that there is only one way for this to take place. The infant has "symbolized," or created an impression in his mind, of an object no longer present to his senses.

This development is called "object-constancy," the holding of an object as a "constant" internally, and is considered the end of infancy and the beginning of childhood.[5] The development doesn't take place in a cumulative, piecemeal fashion, as further intellectual development *will*. Just as in the "goggle experiment" mentioned in the first chapter, object-constancy seems suddenly to occur as an all-inclusive form of knowing and perceiving. This ability to create a symbol, or mental substitute for a real stimulus, is a major step in adapting to the world.[6]

Imitative word play between infant and mother often precedes object-constancy, but meaningful language comes *after* this development of symbolic ability.[7] Then the name for a thing can become *denotative,* pointing toward or "standing for" an object just as the symbol does.

The child first names things in his direct line of sight. Naming is initially a kind of visual-aural "grasping for" the object. (Ask a tiny child to say *hand,* and he will move his hand as he says the word.) Later, name labeling can be attached to symbols—that is, a name can be given something not immediately present to the senses. Naming is then a "symbol-for-a-symbol," a *double-substitution.* Eventually the original symbol can be dismissed, the word label being sufficient for intellect's reality interaction. At this point reality is twice removed, however, and this is the beginning of abstraction.

Through cultural conditioning, the name label for a thing will become, over time, a specific *intermediary*, functioning between the sensory input and the finally created percept—that which is "seen." The acculturated person doesn't just "see the tree," for instance, but the tree-as-named. And through acculturation, a name doesn't simply denote. Language becomes *semantic,* which means that the name or word carries with it the related attitude sets of that culture. This has far reaching effects.

Any object, symbolized or not, that has been labeled with a name, then has this mediation-effect of semantics to funnel through before being cognized by the acculturated mind. Whether the sensory stimulus is from out-there, as with a tree, or internally generated, as with its symbolic form, the stimulus is channeled through the mediating act of "the tree as named," that is, language and its semantic overlay.

Jerome Bruner spoke of our "representing reality to ourselves" verbally in order to make metaphoric mutations of our representations and so change aspects of that reality. This is one of the uses of language and creative logic. But, through acculturation, we don't employ language selectively—either as a tool for logic, or as communication. When language becomes semantic, and takes on negative and positive values beyond denotation, our homeostatic system reacts to the emotional undertones involved. Then we act on tangible sensory data, as well as our abstract creations, *through* our culture's value system. No longer do we interact directly with reality, neither a reality of the natural world, including other people, nor the reality of creations possible through creative logic. We interact with a "mediated reality" and consider the artificial result our natural condition.

When semantic mediation overrides our direct reality interaction in this way, as severe a breakdown in biological phasing occurs as you find in sleep-walking, hallucination, or *delerium tremens*. And, when our sensory-perceptual system is finally channelled entirely through the semantic grid, somewhere in adolescence, a condition of accepted, "normal lunacy" results. The shift from the reality of childhood to the fantasy of cultural life is then largely complete.

Intelligence develops in the child by interactions with concrete life-processes.[8] Logical growth means increasing one's *capacity* for such reality interaction.

Logic grows in the child by active participation with real things. *Practical Intelligence,* as Piaget calls it (I see the object; pick up the object; avoid the object; etc.) builds an expanding basis for "operational thinking," when the child starts combining his learned responses into more complex interactions. These "combinational forms" of thinking expand continuously too, until the child finally becomes capable of "operational thinking" (performing creative operations on his reality data), that is *not tied to* specific concrete situations.[9] Somewhere between his fifth and sixth years, the child learns to create *abstract* constructs, that is, synthesize possibilities "in his head" that have *no* reference to object or symbols. He can then interact with his own creation, and with a logical consistency.

This is a critical point of life. It is not fortuitous that this is the period in which most literate cultures begin the serious cultural training of their children. For at this sixth-year stage, the child can create *concepts* along abstract lines. He can then transact with reality through patterns having no concrete reality associations. Until this stage the child could only interact with actual, tangible things and events. Since abstract notions could *not* be grasped, fear and anxiety, for instance, could only be reacted to or projected out, and so warded off to some extent.

Once the child can deal with abstract logic, his cultural conditioning goes into high gear. "Education" begins. And from the moment the child can logically deal with such an abstract phenomenon as anxiety, he automatically begins the construction of his *own* concepts based on cultural anxieties. He makes this creative move *unconsciously,* with the same complete biological involvement all conceptual structuring requires, and of straight *necessity*—in order to survive the expectancies of his culture.

This marks the end of childhood—the end of the "innocent acceptancy of the given without question." Once high-level combinational forms evolve, and the mind can conceptualize abstractions, the "given" of nature is never again "accepted without question." *Nor should it be,* necessarily. For at this point the child can begin to interact creatively to *transform* the given. He can transform the given through the higher forms of creative logic then unfolding. But such transformation is hardly the reason for the end of innocence. Rather the opposite; the reason lies primarily with the culturally induced fear and anxiety, those twins of doubt that split one's communion, and fragment one's life into isolation. There is a vast difference between creatively interacting with the flow of nature to transform it—*that for which creative logic was developed by life*—and creating a *buffer* to that nature out of fear. And yet logical thinking is used for both creative acts.

To say that operational thinking is entering its "mature stage" at age six hardly means that the child's mind is "matured," or that the highest forms of operational thinking are *functional* at this point. It means that the highest forms of operational thinking are *capable* of *development* at this stage. (Logical growth is roughly chronological, just as sexual growth.) To be developed, as a creative interaction with reality, creative logic must be so *employed*. And even so, the manner of employment determines the manner of development.[10]

"Propositional logic," for instance, is a way by which the mind can "feed its reality data into a set of possible hypotheses *compatible* with the data." Through this operational form the child can combine reality data in a variety of ways, all "in his head."[11] Our culture fosters this operation by our schooling. But our methods quite naturally also channel and restrict the usage and development according to culturally acceptable patterns, shifting the function from direct reality to semantic reality.

Consider the highest form of all operational thinking, called *Reversibility Thinking.* According to Piaget this is the most complex interaction with reality possible, and the rarest of our mental acts.[12] (And yet this formal operation of mind becomes functionally possible during this sixth-year period.)

Reversibility Thinking is the ability to "hypothetically consider any state along a continuum of possibility as potentially equal to any other state, and return to the same state from which the proposed operation began.[13]

Reversiblity Thinking is the operation of intellect found in those great scientific Eureka! creations, those rare landmarks of mind on which much proliferating nonsense is often built. Reversibility Thinking is found in great art, and in the nonordinary reality interactions of don Juan and Jesus.[14]

Cultural conditioning assures that most of us *never* "consider any state along a continuum of possibility as equal to any other state." Cultural conditioning makes it unlikely that we ever consider anything outside the confines of cultural acceptancies.

Consider the effect *should* our creative mind act on reality as suggested in Reversibility Thinking. Don Juan's life, for instance, exemplifies such a mode of interaction in an integrated experience. And below are some examples of fragmented forms of this function occurring spontaneously. Bear in mind that Reversibility Thinking forms as a possible function (developed or not) somewhere around the sixth year, and generally atrophies as an open-ended possibility, through neglect and inhibition, somewhere around adolescence. Consider the following:

Yuri Geller, as a source of phenomena, is controversial. I don't wish my argument to be contingent on reports made by those enthusiasts writing about Geller, or on Geller's *own* evaluations of his strange ability. In my notes to this chapter I explain my reasons for both this qualification and my willingness to use Geller as an example.[15] For the point is, whimsical, subtle, and *unreliable* as the phenomenon might be, Geller *can* bend forks, coins, keys, and such, without touching them. And he discovered his ability at *age seven,* when he found he could influence the running of his watch. Over the years he expanded his ability, devoting it to stage-show displays.

Recently, in television tests in Britain and on the Continent, Yuri invited his television audiences to participate in his performance by holding forks themselves, there in their homes, while he performed on the screen. His idea was that should there be a latent ability of such a nature in others, some viewers might experience their forks bending when Yuri's did. Of some thirty thousand estimated viewers in the British event, some fifteen hundred reported that indeed this happened. And all of those successful participants were between the ages of *seven* and *fourteen.* The age factor is, of course, the point of significance.

The poltergeist phenomena, which I will dwell on again, nearly always occurs in connection with a young person somewhere around or shortly before adolescence.

Balinese child "trance-dancers," always girls in

that particular culture, become capable of trance-dancing around *seven years of age.* At that point they can, as can the adult women, dance over hot coals without harm.

Ernest Hilgard, of Stanford University, writes that the child is not capable of trance ability until somewhere around age seven, and most people, in western cultures at least, lose their trance ability somewhere around early adolescence. (Only an estimated 20 percent seem to retain the capacity for deep trance after that, and most are unaware of having the ability, even so.)

Operational thinking of such complexity as Reversibility Thinking becomes possible somewhere after the sixth-year stage mentioned. To be *utilized,* as one of intellect's ways for interacting with the real world, it would have to be employed, put to practice, *as were all other forms of operational thinking,* in the first formative years.

For a variety of reasons, some of which will be explored in the following chapters, this ability to "consider any possibility in a continuum of possibility as equal to any other state" is channeled into the abstract forms of semantic-cultural logic. And as the higher forms of intellect are *employed,* so they develop. When devoted to semantic and cultural logic, they unfold accordingly. This is why cultural logic can only *follow,* though in close parallel with, the chronological development of the intellect. Studies show that the preadolescent begins to function according to cultural logic (or begins really to respond as a "reality-adjusted" person) somewhere around nine or ten years of age. Trance temporarily suspends the cultural channeling, and opens creative logic again to considering any possibility in a continuum of possibility.

(Piaget speaks of the preadolescent "reality adjustment" as the final fading of "magical thinking," or "autistic thinking," and the beginnings of true maturation. The inevitable and understandable bias of Piaget's cultural assumption doesn't undermine the value of his work nor its *relevance to* my completely opposite argument.)

Language and logic grow apace, and the beginnings of a semantic reality coincide with the emergence of "propositional logic" since the semantic construct *is* a logical abstraction. Even so, the real gist of the semantic reality can't be *given* the child. We try to "educate" him accordingly, but he will automatically construct the abstract concepts on which culture is *based,* and quite unconsciously. He *must* construct such concepts *in order to survive our reality.* (If he didn't, we would have to put him away.) His whole biological process responds as automatically as it has all along. Survival is the issue. And in responding to his survival needs, the child *creates culture anew.*

(We are currently witnessing in both Europe and America a striking increase in childhood "autisms," or refusals and/or inabilities to make reality adjustment. This is attributed to the inordinate complexity, confusion, and contradiction inherent in our present-day social scene.)

So the crucial shifting of the child's interaction with a world of living process to interaction with a semantic reality must, of necessity, await the necessary logical development of mind. Even so, the construction of the semantic reality is a long slow process for the same reason that the development of operational thinking was a slow process. The intellect develops by activity. And a system designed for interaction with a real world of living process finds interaction with abstractions more difficult and less attractive. Our higher forms of logical processing are demanded for the task, and yet that for which the processes were biologically developed is ignored and inhibited. The child adopts consensus thinking largely through fear—but he must be *motivated,* which means literally *driven,* to adopt the abstractions of our current literate and abstract orientation.[16]

Understand that the child trance dancer can't dance over coals until around age seven because to walk fire and not be burned is a *high level form of combinational thinking,* just as bending forks by "thought." The mind is then entertaining a "continuum of possibility in which any state is equally possible." (The fact that the resulting reality mirrors the activity was explained in my book, *Crack.*)

Were "practical intelligence," which simply *responds* to the real world, the only intellectual operation in effect, the Balinese child would be severely burned. Were her "propositional logic," or Reversibility Thinking channeled into *our* forms of semantic structuring, then, equally, the child would be burned. The hypothesis of *not* being burned is given by her culture, and when able to grasp the hypothesis, she responds accordingly. The act is not "intellectual" in our specialized use of the term. It is intellectual in the sense of *interaction* with reality—neither just response to nor reaction to. She "sees and does"; she learns by imitation. Those responding to Geller's phenomenon by "bending forks" themselves, were following the same pattern. Their ego "roof-brain" had nothing to do with it (and they also hadn't *yet* learned fully enough that the act was impossible). Don Juan might consider this their "body-knowing." All of it is "intellect," thinking, operations of the mind.

At any rate, language becomes dominant in the mind-body-reality relationship because, among many things, of its ability to convey the positive and negative judgments and values of society–that is, because of the semantic factor of language. And once the verbal logic of a culture dominates the intellect, the semantic context becomes the formative matrix within which the higher forms of intellect are functional. Any mature form of logic (free of subjectivity and emotional overlay) is then rare. A verbalized form of logic is employed on every hand, though, the form fitting the needs of culture.

In the following chapters the effects of acculturation on the growing personality will be explored. Each isolated effect as presented might not stand alone with much conviction. But these strands will weave in and out, and a more convincing fabric may form–perhaps a net with which to catch some glimpse of "not-doing," and even "stopping the world."

3. Prediction and Control

The thrust of any culture, archaic or contemporary, is to predict and control the flow of nature. Prediction and control in this sense are intellectualized forms of our survival drives, and misuses of our capacity for transformation. Prediction and control could be potent, logical tools. In their acculturated form they set us against, and split us from, the flow of life, and defeat us in our very attempts to understand our nature and respond intelligently.

In archaic cultures man controlled his own acts, through myth, ritual, and taboo, to mirror his concept of nature. By this he tried to assure himself a nature of predictable order.

Contemporary culture attempts to predict and control a nature conceived as hostile. In turn, each of us, *lest* we be "natural," and thus hostile, must be predicted and controlled for the sake of the social body. Potential hostility underlies our interaction with both our reality and our self. In the (hostile) reality resulting, our homeostatic system can never relax, nothing is stable, and our "flight-fight," or "startle" system is on a perpetual alert; everything seems threatening.

Ordinarily our "startle system" should be activated only by actual disruptions of our homeostatic system. Homeostasis is like an electronic burglar-alarm circuit. So long as our feeling of stability and security is undisturbed, our startle system is quiet. A break in our sameness, or unsureness of outcome, rings the alarm.

Our "startle system" retains its natural function, but gets overlaid by cultural conditioning. For instance, I am walking back to my car, arms loaded, and must squeeze past a recently parked station wagon. Suddenly, inches from my face, a huge German police dog lunges, fangs bared, slaughter sounds roaring forth. Immediately, every fiber of my being is alerted, my heart plunges, and my leg muscles fire into propulsion.

As quickly, my scanning devices note the "thank-God safety glass" twixt me and the beast, and I stop trying to push my molecules through those of my car. The entire procedure takes the flick of an eyelash. I was a "bit startled," is all.

Actually, that is never all. I will check station wagons in the future before getting too close, at least until the incident fades. All too often I will carry the incident over in "tape-looped" imaginings, structuring up a rich fabric of resentment toward owners of police dogs and station wagons. This is my reflective intellect's acculturated response—to an experience in which it *played no part.* For my conscious thinking is too slow for decision making and action taking of this sort. Conscious thinking can only follow this "bodyknowing." (The "knee-jerk reaction" of a singed finger is "un-thought," in this sense, but we generally dwell on it quite a bit after the fact.)

Acculturation links our homeostatic system to our social-ego thinking in disruptive ways. This slower-minded *me,* here in my "roof-brain," is designed to be *informed by* my startle system. Acculturation rather *reverses* this natural order, and my "roof-brain" starts informing my startle system. And the natural, one-way street of the startle effect gets its traffic snarled when ego-me tries to take over the whole operation, rushing backward as well as forward.

Survival learning and "body-knowing" depend on remembering "traumas" and making comparison evaluations with new experience. This homeostatic process operates below roof-brain awareness. Through reflective thinking, however, we remember, compare, and then try to *preconstruct* events before they can happen. This is a perfectly logical and practical way to *avoid* trauma and even death. Culture is based on this perfectly logical assumption. And entering into an event to restructure it *is* one of the uses of operational thinking. (In *Crack,* for instance, I used fire-walking as a most extreme and dramatic example of this kind of restructuring.) The problem lies with the proper use, or "biological phasing," of this form of creative logic. In what way do we "accept the given without question," *or* transform the given? What are the criteria for transformation?

Intellectualizing the flight-fight performance converts the rare startle experience into a chronic anxiety. This conversion largely defeats that for which the system was designed.

Rabbit, for instance, would have avoided the station wagon in the first place. He would have known of the dog before getting there.

Since *my* reality is *semantic,* constantly reinforced by the chatter in my "roof-brain," near disaster must break upon me full force to penetrate the artificial "stable sameness" churning around in my word-filled head.

Intellectualizing the homeostatic and flight-fight system places a past-future grid on all present-moment reality. Prestructuring events becomes the pattern for transactions with reality. We start conceptually putting our present reality data together according to preconstructed notions of what the *future* should be. Body-knowing, no longer trusted or heeded, seems to atrophy, and as pointed out, our possibilities for creative interaction get sharply curtailed.

The mind-body system has a natural division of labor. Culture disrupts this scheme. The homeostatic system gets intellectualized, and the intellect gets locked into homostatic reactions to any proposed break in "stable sameness." The "semantic reality," sustained in our roof-brain activity, then mediates between our senses and our percepts. Such mediation creates the illusion of predicting and controlling an infinitely contingent universal system.

To the culturally conditioned mind, any other way of dealing with the world seems madness. Trust is impossible to the conditioned mind. For instance, don Juan attempted to get Carlos to trust his "body-knowing" and run in unknown wilderness in the dark. This kind of "surrendering" runs counter to every facet of acculturation–as don Juan well knew. It involves the complete opposition of prediction and control.

Rabbit-in-the-wilds will hop right over sleeping fox who is well fed, but rabbit will give *hungry fox,* sleeping or no, a wide berth. How does rabbit know? (The Zen swordmaster cannot be caught unawares. Don Juan always seemed to know when Carlos was coming to visit.)

Carlos tried to trip don Juan with "what-ifs," *What-if* a man with a high-powered rifle with telescopic sight were lying in wait to kill him, what would don Juan do *then?* Why, he simply wouldn't *be* in such a place. But what if the man were *hiding,* in secret, with a long-range rifle, how could don Juan . . . ? Carlos argued from the grounds of one separated from his natural communion with life.

But, even the slowest will point out, rabbits in the wild *do* get caught–that "well-fed fox" probably *fed* on one. True, and that is as it has to be, for rabbit and fox. There is, however, a qualitative, functional difference between rabbit and man. What this fundamental difference is can't be grasped, however, much less developed, by man, until that larger relationship with life, as *displayed* by rabbit (and don Juan) is *regained* by man.

(The romantic sentiment that the death of rabbit to fox is "woodland tragedy" is an outgrowth of our cultural death concept in one of its guises, mixing memory, sentiment, and death into its treacly substitute for life. The event of death is not a tragedy—to rabbit, fox, or man. But the *concept* of death *is* a tragedy, for man, and *indirectly,* for poor fox, rabbit, bush, bird, just anything and everything in man's path.)

In the first chapter I listed several examples of homeostasis. There are many subtle aspects of the system. For instance, the body apparently has a "memory system" that is not directly cerebral, or "in the head." Various parts of the body seem to act as "memory banks" for other parts of the body. The life experience of one's leg, for instance, may be sustained as a memory in other parts of the body. There are evidently hundreds of nexus points, cross-indexing between the parts of the body. A low muscle-tone vibration, stilled only in the deepest stage of sleep, may keep the interlocking information continually active, give a stable unity to the diverse body parts, and make available to the "startle system" the material needed for those lightning quick sensory evaluations.

Consider that a toe suffers some injury. The trauma is "registered" in the body for comparison with future data. Should a similarity in incoming data appear, the body acts to ward off a repetition. Suppose that thumb, rather than toe, meets a similar condition. Thumb doesn't have to send a dossier to toe or brain to await computation and eventual reply. Toe's report of the trauma is filed in other repositories, quickly available throughout the network.

Should a limb or portion of our body be lost, its memory-bank deposits continue to register as data in the cognitive scheme. The homeostatic system keeps its stable unity intact as well as continuing the availability of the experience carried therein.

In phantom-limb pain, for instance, a previous trauma occurring to toe might start causing discomfort months after one's entire leg had been amputated. Many amputees continue to "feel" their lost limbs, and this was long a medical mystery. Acupuncture can relieve such pain by locating the point in the body in which these particular "memories" are stored, or, if the "gate theory" is correct, are relayed on to the brain.[1]

Ida Rolfe's system of massage seems to break up some traumas attached to "body" memories. Often nerve-muscle hangups that curtail areas of the body can thus be eliminated. Sam Keen wrote of an area of his chest that was affected by a trauma. When this area was "Rolfed," Keen found himself "reliving" a painful experience from childhood in which emotional catastrophe had been linked with a specific injury to his chest.

In the body's homeostatic procedures, other muscles partially take over the functions of an injured area, to promote healing. On reactivation of the injured area, the trauma of the experience may tend to reactivate as well, bringing on anxiety. As a result it happens occasionally that the "relief" function of the other muscles never completely relinquishes the "emergency role-playing." Over the years there might be, for example, a slight "hitch" in the way the shoulder is carried.

John Lilly gave a similar report on the "Rolfing" of scar tissue from an injury received from an axe in his college days. As the "Rolfing" broke down the tie-up within his foot, he relived the entire experience in a "sensory-perception replay."[2]

(Through the extremities of Rolfing, these complexes are broken up, apparently cleaning house. Purgative but not preventative, periodic repetitions of the performance seem necessary. I am reminded of Jesus' parable of the demon being exorcised from a body and wandering about the countryside with no place to stay. Quietly he crept back to his old abode and found it swept clean. So he rushed out, gathered all his kin, and took over the body again. Which body, of course, was then worse off than before.)

Any interaction with reality is "thinking" on some level. Much thinking takes place below conscious awareness. The few examples given here and in the first chapter indicate the depth and tenacity of the body's homeostatic drive. Once developed, this can no more be easily changed than can any other aspect of our physique. Recent studies suggest that the "minor hemisphere" of the brain might be directly connected with such nonaware or "unconscious" processes, a matter to which I will return. Enough for now to point out that the desire for a stable sameness of the known and familiar acts on the entire organism, including our conscious processes. Many "rational" decisions, apparently reached through logical processes, are reactions to this "nonaware" dynamism. Surface cognition is intricately tied with autonomous function.

As I outlined in *Crack,* we used to think of our cognitive system, with its elaborate sensory apparatus, as a kind of telephone switchboard, bringing in messages from out-there and assembling them into a reasonable facsimile within. We know now that our cognitive process is hardly so passive. Our notions of what is "real" function as an "editorial hierarchy of mind," deciding which data, among all available, is "fit to print" as perceptual events. This conceptual framework even "sends out orders" to its sensory reporters for the *kinds* of material desired by the current newsroom synthesis policy. This policy is our "world view," the result of the preprogramming of culture, organizing our cognitive system along set patterns of response.

Cultural conditioning disrupts the division of labor between intellect and survival. Then cultural logic brings about an artificial kind of "verbal agreement" between these basic functions so split. The result is a concept of general threat that embraces every aspect of reality.

Much of our "body-knowing" is lost to us through this intellectual overlay. In the first chapter I described an experiment by Charles Tart which indicated what "body-knowing" might encompass. Rabbit and don Juan also give tangible examples and offer insight into our original "communion state." This state of early childhood should have been vastly enhanced, expanded, and creatively entered into through the development of operational thinking. Instead, our natural communion was thwarted and driven underground. As we get isolated from our childhood relation with the Flow, our homeostatic system, designed for survival in a living process, gets converted to our ego-image survival in a world of semantics. The more the homeostatic drive is channeled into the cultural process, the greater the loss of communion.

The child rejects hostility, if possible, and projects his fear outside himself as best he can. To project his fear outwardly he erects barriers to that fear. A barrier or "buffer" to fear insulates the child from the real world as well as from the nonreal abstractions of fear. Isolated and fragmented, intellectual attempts to predict and control are *substituted* for the security and "knowing" of being one with the flow of life. Thus our semantic prism, standing *for* the world, acts as mediant between our senses and our percepts.

The semantic universe resulting is "logically coherent" within its own logic. This logic is a response to the death concept, however, based on avoidance of death. A permanent, ceaseless undercurrent of threat-without-known-cause, or threat from hypothetical future-cause, keeps the homeostatics drive anchored to the social-semantic. This alliance is "below the limen of awareness" and simply happens to us.

"Reality-adjusted" thinking is cultural thinking. Our accepted concepts define our common-sense reality, and common sense means sensory responses held in common. And the only way we know in which responses are so held is through our language structure. To mature culturally is to learn to see, taste, touch, hear, smell, according to a verbal consensus.

A literate culture such as ours is preserved by a verbal flexibility unknown to archaic cultures. This flexibility in no way changes the underlying function of prediction and control. Instead, our fearful desire is offered an endless new array of illusions that it *can* predict and control.

Archaic cultures organize around perfectly remembered myths and legends that outline the actions sustaining the culture. Variations of the given are extremely limited. The Trobriand Islander is confused when challenged with "obvious contradictions" in his cultural logic. He resorts to the best rationale of which he is capable or goes blank. But he keeps his world view intact. Questioning his ontological constructs never occurs within his closed society. No flexible system of rationale is developed, since none is needed.[3]

In literate societies this is not the case. A written language grows increasingly ambiguous. The flexibility of our current semantic reality is extensive. Endless metaphoric mutation can occur within our process without in the least disturbing the *function* of culture. To be acculturated to a literate world is to develop an infinite capacity for rationalization. (Rationale is our cultural parody of Reversibility Thinking, perhaps.) Writing down our abstractions gives an increasingly flexible rationale.

Functional change, however, is not possible for any aspect of culture. The sound and fury of our current metaphoric mutation gives the illusion of newness and change, but the function of culture remains the same. In our culture, the priests are continually being overthrown, changing vestments and creed, proclaiming new ages to the excited audiences. But this eternal game of "king-of-the-wood" changes culture not at all.

Our cognitive system, with its complex sensory network, is a great synthesizer. Not infallible, it can be tricked or trick. In one sense, we have no cognitive process, as acculturated people, but only a recognitive one. I believe that poet Blake had learned to cognize. And I suspect that Carlos Castaneda was being trained by don Juan to cognize as well as re-cognize. To cognize may require a relinquishment of those most tenacious drives for prediction and control.

Academic assumptions have convinced us that we have survived by *intellectually outwitting* the forces of nature. This assumption perverts every facet of that which makes us human into "economic-adaptive necessities," and is not the case. We have survived, in fact, in spite of such cultural channelings of intellect, channelings that have consistently turned our Eden into our hell.

Our enormous brain is not a "survival mechanism." The cockroach is far older than man, obviously "better adapted," and will probably be around long after we are gone. Life has developed our "oversized brain" for the same reason we probably "overdeveloped" our sexual parts–simply for the joy of exploring the capacities suggested therein.

4. Feeding and Feedback

Monkeys have been removed from their mothers by caesarian section, raised without contact with other monkeys, and then placed in a cage with one side a rear-projection screen. On this screen will be projected pictures and movies of children, landscapes, and animals. All of these draw only a "ho-hum" from monkey; but flash a picture of another *monkey* on that screen and instantly the captive, who has never seen one of his own kind, reacts excitedly, trying to get through to that other monkey. Cognition of one's species seems to be genetic in the higher mammals.

Monkey raised in isolation proves to be fearful and will not explore new objects. If given even a "surrogate" mothering-one, a mock-up of approximate monkey dimension and the source of food, young monkey will then make exploratory forays into his ambient, returning to the surrogate as home-base, his touchstone for homeostatic security.

Moving from the known to the unknown is the basis of learning for monkey as well as human, and anxiety and fear block the ability to risk the unknown in both.

That the human infant is also born with an innate recognition of his own species was briefly outlined in chapter two. Face cognition gave an anchor point for the cognitive process and led to object-constancy, imitation, exploration, and growth of intelligence.

Watch a nursing infant and you will find that his eyes stay glued on the "mothering-one's" face. Little by little his vision moves out, returning always to the point of stability. The homeostatic effect of this cognition pattern leads to adoption of the world view of one's society. Consider also that the face-for-focus and the intake of nourishment are intimately associated from the beginning. Nourishment means survival, which links with homeostasis just as the face-recognition pattern. Further, as Jung spoke of the child as "living in the unconscious of the parent," the value system and psychological set of the "mothering-one" links also with homeostasis, food, survival, and so on. Studies with congenitally deaf children show that extensive world view information is perceived nonverbally.

Language development is a paralleled but separate act from logical growth. Consider, though, that language and physical survival are linked from birth. As the infant locks on the mothering-one's face, his source of nourishment, he tunes in to a nonstop flow of words. The infant's own lalling sounds are picked up by parents and incorporated into a language-learning process. Mamma and dadda, for instance, are infant lalling sounds picked up and used by parents as "names" for immediately associable objects, in the parents' desire to have the infant respond linguistically.

Imitation is one of the strongest and earliest learning devices.[1] Imitation, which is a form of play, is the preliminary to symbolic formation. Mother imitates baby's lalling sounds, baby eventually identifies and repeats accordingly. This mirroring helps generate the language function. Within months a great imitative game results. Imitation is both play and a source of positive feedback from the mothering-one. The rewards of this combination prove a steady stimulus to language development, for the feedback comes from the source of nourishment.

The words of others, with all their approvals and disapprovals, enter into the structuring of the child's world. The homeostatic system learns to respond semantically since words convey the psychological emotional states of those providing nourishment. Language growth incorporates the criteria scheme of parent and thus culture.

Semantic structuring will slowly become the survival criteria of the growing person. This will lead to an eventual shift of data from the real world to data from a semantic reality. The "socially mature" sensory system lives in, and reacts to, a word-built world. As the imprinting of culture assumes dominance, hypothetical extrapolations, logical fears, and ideological phobias become the abstract issues of flight-fight and survival.

Language play is one of the child's ways for exploring reality.[2] The child's paradign for naming-imitation is the parent. Negatives and positives are inevitably carried within language, but this effect is fended off by the child. The parental concept of a hostile universe nevertheless becomes operative in the child along with his development of operational thinking.

Until operational thinking can create abstract concepts and interact according to them, the unity of the child's communion state holds.[3] His unity with life holds even though fear and anxiety are elements within it.

The child is forced to create concepts according to his cultural pattern, just as he had to form an "object-constancy" for a stable world. From his base of object-constancy he could then form a picture of the world through his explorations--explorations that were his growth of operational thinking. When the child's operational thinking can create abstractions and concepts built on abstractions, he begins the formation of cultural concepts in order to survive in that context. This marks the end of childhood.

The beginnings of cultural concept formation is the beginning of the formation of the social self. The child turns to peers, since the cultural concept is built on a semantic consensus. No longer do two children just share the same stage of play–they try to share the same script, and problems arise. To create the semantic concept is to interact with reality accordingly. So the "other"–who shares the semantic construction and so is its content–must be sought out, acknowledged, complied with, accommodated, and incorporated into one's play. (Play is still reality exploration for the preadolescent, even though it shifts from a natural world to a semantic consensus of other people.)

Reality exploration after age six is subject to the open-ended interactions of operational thinking. Consider, however, that the child has projected fear and anxiety outside his self from the beginning. An open-end, unknown exploration thus includes a world of out-there fears. The intricate web of culture spins a veil over this openness and offers a word-built agreement of the known to act as buffer against the unknown. The young person willingly turns to social and semantic exploration, both as escape from an infinite openness, and as part of his automatic tendency to imitate in his play.

The turn to the social-semantic is a turning from the communion state of childhood. The child's loss of primary perception parallels his development of that social self-system demanded by culture. This splits the child mind between an inner and outer and separates him gradually from cognizance of his unity with the flow. The creation of the social ego parallels the construction of the semantic universe. The new self-system splits from the innocent acceptancy and dependence on "the given," and is forced into an increasing dependence on culture as a "surrogate."

Positive-negative feedback is one of the principal ways by which the split between subject and object takes place. (A self-system can develop distinct from others without inflicting a sense of alienation. Preliterate and archaic cultures show individuality with a minimum of isolation. We presume they have no individuality since we equate being an individual with being alienated.) Infant development is locked into reactions to the evaluation scheme of parent-provider. A good-bad judgment system seems inevitable. Even animal mothers bat their young about for correction.

In acculturation, however, the criterion at stake is almost never just the physical well-being of the infant or child. The issue at stake is the parental need for verification of their own life investment, their own world view, their own passions and commitments, and their own images-of-self in a social criteria-set. Failure of one's child to verify one's own world view by proper response is a world threat as well as social-image threat. For any of us, nonagreement threatens our ideation and our identity placement. This is uniquely so in our relations with our children.

The parental criteria system is ambiguous and shifting. Adaptation to that system is tentative and transient at best. There is no "homeostatic" stability in the world of opinions and judgments of others. For an infant or child, negative feedback from the source of nourishment is a survival threat. Both parent and child "scan and sort" their reality data according to positive feedback, in a homeostatic flight-fight interplay, though from markedly different sets. The infant and child's set is egocentric, centered within, and his needs are direct and unambiguous. The parental set is determined by a context of others-out-there which never clarifies, and ambiguity is the rule.

As found in the example of nursing, the psychological effect can outweigh the physical. Anything that implies anxiety or hostility will be rejected by the infant, if possible. Once some separation between "I and not I" takes place through object-constancy and symbol formation, psychological "projections" onto an out-there become the response to fear and anxiety.

The child hears himself referred to as "good-me" for certain actions, and as "bad-me" for others. He reacts to "bad-me" accusations in two ways: he may try to avoid the actions involved, and/or he may "project" the bad-me onto a "not-me" that is out-there. This is the rudiment of lying and leads to the development of the social self.

Language may carry negative undertones automatically, but language learning wins the greatest reward from semantically oriented parents. "Good-me" learns the language even though the semantic overtones and undertones carry guilt, anxiety and hostility. Such irrational contradiction impinges on the child increasingly.

The child will project the irrational as best he can, just as he would reject an "anxiety-ridden nipple" earlier. He projects the negative outwardly to hold to his interior wholeness. To avoid the fragmenting anxieties he adopts an "as-if" *pose of outward compliance.* This pose depends on verbal communication, which in turn entails the entire *semantic* act, the criteria-set of those with whom he must communicate.

A myriad of combinations are possible for synthesis within the cognitive system. But those combinations in agreement with the value system of the parent-providers are given positive reinforcement. The cognitive system of the infant and child develops around the cognitive scheme of the parents as a biological, survival procedure.

Equally the child learns to damp down and eventually eliminate functions and phenomena not corresponding with parental sets. The "quasi-hallucinatory" world of the infant and child gradually restricts to those syntheses given word sanction by parents and superiors.

Name labeling gives social sanction whether that labeling is "positive" or "negative." To the cultural process positives and negatives are equally functional. There is a sharp distinction, however, between phenomena given negative identification, and phenomena not named at all. For no names are given to those phenomena that are not *acceptable* to the cultural function. And if there is no name given, there is no *identity,* no stable-place in the reality frame. Unplaced phenomena are then *threats* to the stability of the known. The homeostatic system will eventually screen out their occurrence as best it can.

Thus the turn to consensus reality after age six is doubly binding. The cognitive system matures in response to a semantic scheme of identification. The mature person recognizes according to the patterns of the cultural language-cognition system. Through acculturation we equate our individual survival with our cultural survival, until life and death become matters of verbal concept. The acculturated person then has, as Langer pointed out, an inarticulate fear that his system of ideation might fail and he slip into chaos.

Since maturation is synonymous with the firming up of a semantic value grid, there is then scant possiblity of experiencing noncultural phenomena. The adult lives in a world of culturally acceptable events and shared concepts of what events should be expected. From then on, any nonordinary experience is essentially accidental.

Name labeling, then, leads to semantic overlay, and becomes split-inducing. Realness of phenomena is granted only through name labeling sanctioned by culture; "realness" is thus dependent on the "otherness" of that named "real." Finally, "realness" in a semantic reality is that which separates subject from object, that which splits.

Through cultural conditioning, reality automatically becomes something "alien" to one's true self, one's feeling of identity is fragmented. This is the "world view" by which the social self-system relates to reality. Reality is then an alien construct from which the "self" feels isolated and estranged.

As culturally conditioned people, we are then perpetually stimulated to *wring from* that semantic reality some kind of authenticity for our "alienated self." Our lives grow into one long lament, if not defiant shout of: "Dammit all, I am *here* and I am *real."* We move continually toward a social "identity," a stable placement of our self in a stable sameness of accepted "realness." This is our biological thrust for unity, or homeostasis.

The "identity" we seek, however, can only be sought for in that which has been *identified for us as reality.* And this "reality" in which we seek stable placement is only millions of other equally alienated self-systems also trying to win stable placement in the shifting web of mutual ambiguity. Our homeostatic drive for stability can never achieve its aim in this shifting miasma, chronic anxiety is then the cultural norm.

A heart cell is not lacking in authenticity when working in symbiotic precision and unity. Were it split off from its organic role, it could not function in phase, and would "lose its identity." It would attempt to get back and regain its authenticity as a heart cell. The very notion of authentic or inauthentic, an "identity crisis," could not occur to the cell unless or until it were split off.

The child could not be motivated or driven to cooperate with the irrational aspects of the cultural thrusts were he not first alienated from his native wholeness. "Reality thinking" blocks our symbiotic "body-knowing" and our primary perceptions which are nonsemantic. Our larger sphere of relationship, our natural state of communion with the life-flow system, is by nature *not* separable and cannot be fragmented or categorized. As a result it can't be "named" in any usual semantic sense. The natural unity of self and life is thus "unreal" within the cultural semantic-set that grants "realness" according to semantic sanction. Among the phenomena screened out by the developing child are his unity associations and communication channels.

So culture imposes a split of being; establishes the acceptancies *for* reality, which are all split inducing; and denies the reality of nonverbal experience, and so one's unity with life.

The culture then "offers its services," so to speak, as the source and only source of those possibilities which *might*, if acquired, alleviate or maybe even remove the isolation caused by the culture itself. First you induce the illness, then you sell the remedy.

Through acculturation, verbal channels are all we have left. With these we try to *simulate* our Primary Process of unity and relation. A verbalized form of propositional logic is employed for this, which we call "cultural logic." Cultural logic muddies the nonsemantic logical mode with the ambiguities and subjective emotions of the social set of expectancies. One difficulty with the attempt to simulate a holistic semantic reality through verbal logic is that semantic configurations exist only in the split mind. They are nonexistents within that unified cosmos with which we desire and seek unity. That is, that which we seek is already ours; we are already "there." Our split is imaginary, but "real."

Our desire and need for unity generally remain below our consciousness. Our split of mind always projects our need outwardly and expresses it metaphorically within the social frame. Even the "split of mind" is seen as "out-there." Our move for wholeness is always channeled out-there, into that very cultural energy producing the split. Our internal chaos is seen as chaos out-there needing our attention and ordering. This keeps the culture alive and energetic. Like a fly with one wing, this performance makes a great buzzing, uses much energy, and produces much activity in a tight circle that only repeats itself.

5. Lying

Social-ego begins in a child as a buffer against a web of negative demands. Any demand that the child move outside his egocenter in a unified state is "irrational" to that child, and resisted. The child adopts a "persona mask" to protect his centered existence from the abrasions of the acculturation process. Social-ego is a word-built affair paralleling and imitating the earlier developed self-system much as verbal logic parallels propositional logic. The semantic context places the self as just another object to the demanding otherness of parents, teachers, peers, superiors. By adolescence the world-out-there is the only authentic, the self-in-here isolated from it and fragmented.[1]

Positive reinforcement (you *are* a good child—generally for passivity) gains its power as a release from the possible negative (do that again and I'll . . . —generally for some action.)

Negatives are part of a child's "training," "good for him," vital to his "reality adjustment." He must, after all, live in the world with others. These "others" are trained, of course, to react to the same set of expectancies, and the expectancies based on potential threat create the need for such training to deal with their very results.

As mentioned, many negatives, even those of apparent "life and death urgency," result from the parent's fear of social condemnation. Actions that parent will ignore so long as no one is around are suddenly met with agitated negatives the minute "neighbor" appears. It is neighbor's opinion of parent that is involved, not the child's welfare. Actions of the child are suddenly negated as neighbor appears, and as suddenly ignored again when neighbor leaves. The child's homeostatic response is unable to find the stable-sameness pattern and is confused.

The child finds that he doesn't have to always be, think, or act as demanded. He can, instead, often "shut them up," by simple agreement. The child learns to adopt a *pose of compliance* with the shifting negatives.[2] In a semantic reality, gaining verbal agreement from another is the same as gaining momentary self-verification. And as any child or politician knows, one can give verbal agreement and act differently without attracting too much notice.* Verbal disagreement with another threatens the other's identity or "reality placement," since our reality is semantic.

A child pretends to comply under direct surveillance, and reverts to his "true" or "secret" self the minute he is left alone. He reverts only partially to himself, however, since, once made, the pose of compliance must be sustained to some extent. The outer play of agreement requires more energy and attention

* Note, for instance, that the greater the criminal intent of the politician the more strident his shouts for law and order.

as the demands for conformity increase. And these demands increase in proportion to the child's language ability.

Lying begins as a survival ploy by the child. He attempts to keep his centered balance with the life flow intact. Pretending to be that which is demanded of him produces a "double-mindedness," however, never fully resolved in the mind again.

This "as-if" performance contributes to the growth of roof-brain chatter, or the "internalizing" of the semantic reality.[3] This maneuver will be seen to parallel and imitate the earlier developed object-constancy of the infant world. Roof-brain chatter substitutes the stimuli from the semantic world-of-others and keeps a semantic simulation of that world going at all times.

As part of language development and exploration of his world, a child "talks out his world." He verbalizes his actions, imaginings, and play. Verbalizing is a way of identification of his newly expanding world as well as imitation.[4] Two children playing together will constantly chatter, though neither depends on or expects the other to hear or respond. They simply share the same stage of play. They find no necessity for following the same script, nor have they an audience other than themselves. (Communication with others is a different activity.)

As the child's grasp of language increases, parents and superiors increase their demands for a language-logic response for him. Language facility is mistakenly considered a sign of verbal-logical grasp and "reasoning ability," which it can't be until somewhere between five and six. Conceptual response is always expected prematurely and only adds to the contradictory confusion of compliance demands.

Talking out one's world is frowned on as the "communicative" rather than identifying aspects of language are stressed and expected. Along with a continually growing demand for conformity is a growing demand for silence unless communication is intended.

Kindergarten and schooling complete this demand and enforce it with clear negatives. So the talking out of one's world gets internalized. The internalized language function allies with the "secret self" operating beneath the mask of outer conformity.

The child tries to achieve homeostatic balance and rational continuity within, while coping with the irrationalities and contradictions without. Two aspects of personality must then be attended to, and a confusion of identity grows.

The child's unified, internal world is not recognized by his parent-providers and other superiors. They have long since lost their rapport with their natural communion state and can only respond according to semantic cultural expectancies. They are automatically looking for verification of their own world view, a performance they interpret as guiding the child's "reality adjustment."

The child's outer pose of compliance is accepted as the real. The lying act is all that communicates to "out-there." The child never "thinks any of this through"; his resulting split world simply has no stability. His homeostatic function shifts increasingly toward the semantic placement out-there since his threat syndrome increasingly must gear toward a semantic web of positives and negatives.

Little by little our internalized chatter must reflect more on the outer contradictions, as we try to make the semantic orientation stable. Talking to ourselves inside our heads finally becomes the only reality we are sure of.

Having adopted a protective mask, we eventually forget the "buffer effect" of our pretence. We forget that our lying was an insulation against the accusations and irrationalities of our culture. We finally become, or try very hard to become, our mask itself. This brings on the "will-to-power" stage, when our mode of lying becomes our accepted norm, our unique charm, or "personality." By maturity, our semantic, logical self-system sees itself *as* this mask effect.

Intriguingly, this lying act, so arbitrarily brought about, is an absolute necessity for acculturation. Lying is the necessary response to and for guilting, which is the principle tool for "molding the mind." Attending two contradictory and opposing forces produces ambiguity. In adolescence the mask effect takes over and dominates the system, and "maturity" is the label we give the final dominance of this lying act.

It is not fortuitous that the stages of cultural-logical development coincide with adolescence. The inner life of the preadolescent often coexists with his double-mindedness until genital sexuality begins. Only the "absolutely-other" can meet the needs of this new drive, particularly since culture concentrates on trying to control sex in order to assure cultural adaptation. This contributes to the pull off center. Concentration on the cultural context produces the "norm" of eccentricity. The outer pose of compliance has by then long been given the only placement grant in the semantic reality of the society.

Since lying is essential to guilting, and guilting is the central feature of the cultural process, it is this act that needs exploring. Guilting, however, depends on fear and anxiety, the twin effects of the death concept, which must be dealt with first.

6. The Death Concept

Fear and Anxiety

The death concept never clarifies, but expresses itself as something else. This is the concept's great strength. It expresses as guilt, anxiety, alienation–states of fear giving birth to one another.

A recent study proposed that a child has no "concept" of death until somewhere around eight or nine years of age. A television newscast showed two children around four and six, being led from their home by a social worker. The children had discovered their mother dead on the kitchen floor, but here they were, happily skipping along, holding the social worker's hands, oblivious to "tragedy." "They just don't understand, poor things," was the reaction, but we may rest assured that little by little they will be *taught* to understand.

Children are aware of death as an event, but death as a *concept* requires some logical maturity. For, as with all abstract concepts, this one, too, must be constructed in the mind. Further, to entertain the death concept, the child must have been moved far enough from his natural center to sense an isolation from his primary process. Both of these requirements, conceptual logic and self-isolation, slowly evolve somewhere after the sixth year, becoming firm conceptual patterns by adolescence. Within that period conceptual thinking in abstractions becomes more and more functional. This means also that orientation to the social world becomes functional and the loss of centeredness becomes fixed. The result of these parallel developments is the channeling of operational thinking into verbal logic or "social thinking."

This enforced fusion of functions is brought about through fear. We tend to think of fear as a natural response. This is not the case. *Fright* is a natural response, a biological "startle" effect. But fear is an intellectualized form of this "startle" response.

Earlier I gave the example of a dog in a station wagon "startling" me. This flight-fight signaling system is lightning quick in mobilizing the organism for survival maneuvers. Rabbit-in-the-wild uses "startle" continually, but drops each such episode from consciousness immediately when danger is over.

Our "body-knowing" always retains from each "startle" experience that which is needed for future evaluations. If our conscious mind tried to carry such an elaborate web of memory judgments, our volitional system would be paralyzed. Should rabbit-in-the-wild "intellectually" retain and imaginatively reflect on his startle experiences as we do, *he* would be immobilized and not survive.

Fright is *not* the same as fear. Fear is a learned response. Fear might act as a reflective overlay *on* a startle effect, but fear is an intellectual act we are trained to produce. Fear becomes conceptual, a basic pattern for interpreting reality.

In *Journey to Ixtlan,* Carlos Castaneda gave clear descriptions of suspending his cultural fear-conditioning, and turning his body over to its natural "startle" responses. At one point don Juan either simulated the effect of, or actually attracted, a mountain lion as a specific bodily danger to Carlos' life. Under the impact of his terror, Carlos climbed a cliff in darkness which appeared nearly impossible of access in the light. His body-knowing took over and he possessed powers unavailable to his ordinary thinking.

We express fear in the same way we express all intellectual reflections. Guilt, for instance, is fear over something we have already done. Resentment is fear over something "done to us." Hostility is fear of something being done to us in the present. Anxiety is fear of what might conceivably be done to us in the future. Fear and the "victim mentality" go hand in glove.

Fear is not bodily response to physical survival maneuvers. "Startle" can take care of that. "Startle," or fright, begins to be converted to fear in the child as the child develops logically enough to predict outcomes. By the time a child is three to four years old, logical prediction becomes operational, after a fashion. Then fear begins to develop conceptually. Fear and lying interweave. Any as-if performance, no matter how rationally employed, involves fear.

A child has no criteria other than his experience. As an infant he tasted new objects, since taste was his principal tactile criterion. He rejected "bad tastes" *after* experiencing them. Little by little he *learned* not to repeat certain tastes. And as his possibilities for combinational thinking grew, he developed a criteria synthesized by a cross-indexing of all his senses. Physical tasting was then no longer necessary. He could evaluate "internally" instead of only in sensory-motor ways.

Carl Jung writes that the "child lives in the unconscious of his parents." Consider, instead, that *communion* is our *natural* state. Don Juan, for instance, always knew when Carlos was coming to visit him. People have long been fascinated with Jesus's "paranormal" seeing, "telepathy," clairvoyance, and so on. (And we continually err by thinking we can duplicate these states by arbitrarily developing such effects.)

Consider that the child's state of open communion is not quite the Eden we tend to make of it. For the child's "communion state," in contradistinction with the mature state of a don Juan, for instance, is *open* without qualification. In order to be open to reality the child cannot be closed to the psychological aspects *of* that reality. I have already pointed out how the nursing infant senses anxiety in his "mothering-one," and will reject such a state as best he can.

Anxiety and fear are transferred to the child, in spite of all good intentions, precisely because the child *has no buffers,* no shields or screens of any sort. And fear, as expressed in anxiety, guilt, resentment, and hostility, constitutes a large portion of the adult world. These effects, in turn, furnish a large part of the child's ambient. The child picks up fear as naturally as any part of his experience.

Having no buffers to the fear effect, the child must *learn* fear in order to protect himself from it. Avoidance of fear splits the wholeness, that natural state of communion. This is the "fall."

The child can reject fear only through experiencing it. He can't help but experience it since fear is part of the cultural world of his parents. Little by little he adopts "buffers" to ward off fear. He learns to *fear* fear. Learned fear is the largest contributor, perhaps the only one, to the forced adoption of the *mediant* between sense and percept, the thrust of prediction and control, the avoidance of negative feedback, the persona mask effect, the will-to-power and ace-up-the-sleeve drives, and roof-brain chatter.

Here is the point on which the cultural process falters, but *no one* is "at fault." There are no handy villians toward which we can point the finger of guilt. Nor is there a simplistic reason for this monumental collapse into fragmentation. Should a child not erect buffers to fear, his existence in this fear-filled world would be nightmare. (Perhaps the autistic child fails in his buffer erection and so shuts out reality entirely.) In each of these chapters I try to point up one of the contributing strands in our buffer creation, realizing that I can only glimpse a few overt, inescapably obvious effects. The process of fear is as complex and interwoven a creation as the mind-brain system giving it birth.

None of the few "measle-spot" effects mentioned here offer us avenues for correction of the underlying disease. For culture is a survival-training procedure. The "feral child" shows, by his lack of acculturation, how dependent we are on culture. To lack acculturation would be to lack survival techniques. (We must tend our "misacculturated" in institutions, and put our "malacculturated" in jail.)

Consider, though, that the "feral child" survives in the *wilds*. In civilization he perishes quickly. On examination, culture doesn't equip us so much for physical survival, but for cultural survival. And to be fully "human" is not just to survive physically, but to survive as a cultural creature. Yet the process of becoming fully human is seriously shortcircuited by the process itself.

The problem is one of form and content. Any great work of art or science is a "knowing" of what is form and what is content and how and when to employ each. The letter of the law and the spirit of the law interweave. We have no being except in a mode of being. The mode can stifle or give vehicular expression for the being. Form is the channel for content, and yet tends toward becoming a dam.

A tourniquet, for instance, must be applied in an emergency, to save a life. Not removed, however, the life-saving procedure will produce gangrene and death.

The Pentagon was set up in the midst of a war for survival. Ever since, as with most cultural pursuits, our growing problem is how to survive the "Pentagon effect."

Medicine was evolved, I suppose, as an emergency survival procedure. We must now (it appears) adopt medicine's techniques to survive those very techniques. (For hilarious example: I am told that hospitals now appear to be breeding, in their paranoia concerning "germs," a unique form of pulmonary staph bacteria found nowhere but in hospitals.)

Our problem is to save ourselves from our saviors. The final result of the cultural function of survival training is that most of our lives must be devoted to surviving the culture. The vast bulk of our problems attributed to "man's natural condition" are cultural effects projected into "nature-out-there."

I have based this book on biological drives operating out of balance and out of phase. Surely there are times when "survival" measures are needed. There are, as well, times when other measures are needed than what appears as direct survival. Don Juan teaches

Carlos a "controlled abandon" that is a mixture between naive faith and sophisticated control of one's self.

Bookshelves bulge with new blueprints for cultural corrections, countercultural revolutions, new-consciousness programs, new-age politics, and so on. All this is as it should be. Those asking questions of this nature produce and are offered a wide variety of answers.

A different question begins to form if you take the cultural effect as axiomatic, just as you accept gravity. The antigravity machine is not as yet just around the corner, but we send men to the moon by utilizing the *principles* of gravity. Don Juan insists that Carlos's culture of freeways, jet planes, and universities is Carlos's "hunting grounds." A warrior, in don Juan's sense, changes nothing (except himself.) He utilizes everything, however, and is ultimately responsible for his acts. He assumes "dominion" over his world but then treats every aspect of his life with ultimate concern. This again is abandon, acceptance without question—and control, responsibility for self.

To get back to fear and anxiety, the subject at hand, I will speak of anxiety as "fear without an object," although all fear is an abstraction. When we are "anxious" over the safety of a loved one, for instance, we are projecting "fear" into a future situation that is nonexistent. The "target" of our fear is hypothetical. The "bad happening" we fear is only in our imagination. Once the situation is resolved, the anxiety converts to relief or grief, present states.

Anxiety, as fear without an object, registers in the child as an "empty category." Subtle doubt can split us more effectively than dogmatic assertion. The vague hint filled in by our own imaginative creation can give us our strongest convictions. In the same way, the lack of specific content is what gives anxiety its power. Once formed, this "empty category" is activated through any kind of negative experience, real or imaginary, spoken or unspoken.

The notion of a hostile universe arises from the fact of death. Death is vicarious, however. We build our *concept* of death around our imaginative play on someone else's experience. Our "judgment" against life for "bringing death" is an act of reflective intellect. Our death concept emerges from this judgment and engulfs our universe. From then on our intellect interacts with our reality data according to the formative pattern of a "hostility-out-there."

An inevitable corollary of the assumption of a hostile universe is the notion that any natural process is, of necessity, incomplete and in need of cultural processing and refinement. We consider "natural forces" dangerous and unpredictable unless subjected to intellectual control or guidance. Archaic cultures resort to ritual and taboo for the same reason. In our culture, literacy replaces ritual and guilting replaces taboo. (Functionally there is no difference to culture. Psychologically there is a vast difference.)

Since we consider natural forces potentially hostile until "tamed" by man's intellect, we also consider children to be incomplete, inauthentic, and even potentially dangerous without conditioning. They must, for instance, be taught grief, that they might properly weep at the death of a loved one, lest they be animallike. (We are always on the horns of ambiguity. We look at childhood through heavy overlays of romantic sentiment since that period represents innocence. Yet we never rest until all traces of that innocence have been obliterated and the child made to *understand about life,* and be "realistic.")

Convincing the child of this state of affairs is not easy. The child can't grasp our logical reasoning, not only because abstract logic is undeveloped in the child, but equally because the child's universe is whole and complete. His reality might be impinged upon heavily by fear and anxiety, which he rejects and projects to the best of his ability, but his communion with his world is unbroken since no *buffers* to that unity have been erected.

So in order to make the child understand that life is not the bowl of cherries he seems to think it is, we resort to a specific instilling of fear. We give him "targets" for the automatically sensed anxiety already in him. To force him to attend to our view of reality we resort to a clear spelling out of consequences should he *not* comply with our conditioning demands. These demands prove so contradictory that the child becomes confused concerning stable placement and is more or less forced to eventually accept the accusations.

Since the notion of personal insufficiency is nonconceptual to the young child, all implicit or actual threats are lodged in his general category of anxiety. Psychology has long recognized that anxiety was an "induced" condition, but proposed that since the roots of anxiety are deep, we would have to explore one's "family background" to get at them. This would lead from "mothering-one" to mothering-one in an infinite regress. For anxiety's roots lie in the notion of a hostile universe, and that notion is ancient indeed. Every act of acculturated man reflects the notion of a universal hostility and gives rise to anxiety.

Anxiety appears in the most common-sense attitudes: parents have an initial overriding anxiety over the survival of their child. Then they grow anxious that the child might not achieve reality adaptation; reflect credit on his parents; acculturate well; be an "asset" to his community; and so on. Chronic threat of failure to predict and control, and the consequences of that failure are the web holding society together.

We get glimpses beyond our grids. The explorer Livingstone, for instance, became entranced with Africa and its unknown territory. Carried away with exploring, he would stay out for years without contact with his native land or fellow countrymen. He was not the kind to dine each evening in white tie and tails in the jungle, carrying his culture with him, as Europeans were wont to do. He was not threatened by the unknown and apparently wore his native world view more lightly than some.

One day, leading his party of bearers, Livingstone was attacked by a large lion. The lion seized Livingstone by the shoulder, his teeth going completely through, and shook Livingstone, much as a cat shakes a rat. Livingstone's cognition of the event was crystal clear. He felt the teeth go through, felt the pain and the shock force of the shaking. He knew clearly he was meeting his death.

At no point, however, beyond the first instant's flight-fight startle and initial feeling of pain, did Livingstone again suffer either pain or fear. Quite the contrary—he immediately went into a profound mystic-euphoria, the most impressive event of his life.

His bearers, naturally—else we would not have this marvelous study of death—rushed up at the last instant and killed the lion, Livingstone living to tell the tale. That shoulder did bother him a bit for the rest of his life, but he wrote movingly of his understanding of death. He knew, after that, the *con-*

cept of death, with its prestructurings and imaginations, has no actuality in life. The concept is the tragedy, not the event. He spoke of knowing that within nature life gives itself to life in ways our thinking doesn't grasp.

Wolves, filmed as they were surrounding to bring down a large elk, show an easy grace and playfulness, wagging their tales, relaxed, almost casual. The elk appears, till the very end, haughty and offended. A deer pursued by a mountain lion shows a dogged determination and matter-of-factness, but no "panic" or "fear." The mountain lion shows a definite "play" quality, characteristic of cats. Coyote chasing rabbit reminds one of a pet dog bounding after a stick for retrieval. All animals, on being brought down, appear to die almost instantly, apparently going into immediate shock on losing the chase.

At any rate, bear in mind that Livingstone's experience happened after years in the wilds, traveling essentially alone, and separated from the continual renewal of his cultural concepts. I would suspect that his ordinary world view had become peripheral to some extent, opening him to his primary perceptions.

The "fear of death" may not be so natural a drive as we suppose. Our "survival drive" is not the same as fear. Fright can be linked with survival, but fear is often quite anti-survival. As I outlined earlier with the dog and station-wagon story, fright or startle lasts only seconds and, ordinarily, should be dismissed as quickly. But reflective memory constructs imaginative projects tying in past events, extrapolating and prestructuring into a marvelous array of hypothetical what-ifs concerning the future. *This is not learning.* The body-knowing processes will have already registered the salient features, as needed, to draw on for future flight-fight decision making. And the body will do all this below the limen of roof-brain awareness.

The death concept as a semantic construct mediating between sense and percept can, as stated, be antisurvival. The explorer and writer, John Muir, gave an account of having been "paralyzed" by fear when faced with death. He succeeded, however, in turning his body over to processes beyond his ordinary intellectual grasp. (Don Juan or the Zen Master would have applauded.)

". . . while climbing a sheer face of Mount Ritter, [Muir] found himself '. . . brought to a dead stop, with arms outspread, clinging close to the face of the rock, unable to move hand or foot either up or down. My doom appeared fixed. I *must* fall.

" 'When this final danger flashed upon me, I became nerve shaken . . . and my mind seemed to fill with a stifling smoke. But this terrible eclipse lasted only a moment, when . . . I seemed suddenly to become possessed of a new sense. The other self, bygone experiences, instinct, or Guardian Angel, call it what you will–came forward and assumed control. Then my trembling muscles became firm again, every rift and flaw in the rock was seen as through a microscope, and my limbs moved with a positiveness and precision with which I seemed to have nothing at all to do. Had I been borne aloft upon wings, my deliverance could not have been more complete.' "

Here is an example of "It" breathing one, giving a "positiveness and precision" with which one seems to have nothing to do. This is "body-knowing" in the don Juan sense, possible only when the ordinary grids of fear are somehow by-passed. Fright is a natural alarm signal, alerting and organizing the organism into mobilization. Fear divides, producing confusion.

Anxiety as an empty category can attract any material for its sustenance. It acts as a gravitational field, drawing to itself all the wrongnesses, uneasinesses, vague threats, and disharmonies. Acculturation capitalizes on anxiety for motivating all of us to do that which we will not do naturally or willingly.

The child displays an enormous "open risk" of self in his initial reality explorations. All is an "unknown" to him and he enters into it with joy and trust if *allowed* to. Anxiety retards and checks the willingness to enter the unknown, and yet the child overrides anxiety and fear in his explorations, up to a point—so long as those explorations are with the concrete world.

When operational thinking becomes fully functional, around age six, the child is capable of moving into a continuum of possibility. He is capable of combining reality possibilities, as glimpsed in the few "accidentally occurring" cases given in chapter two. Had he not learned fear, and were he given initial example of reversibility interactions for imitation, as he was given language examples in early childhood, for instance, there would be no limit to the kind of reality or the kind of "self-system" which might result.

Through anxiety and fear our open capacity is channeled into consensus reality thinking, with its verbal logic and orientation to those strictures giving apparent prediction and control..

Ironically, as the ability for combinational logic expands to such open-ended potential as in Reversibility Thinking, the very capacity for abstract logic acts on the long-induced fear and builds anxiety into a concept blocking the thrust toward openness. Fear of the unknown turns the child from his open trust of the cosmos to consensus reality, the peer-group effect, and the semantic system.

And so, in constructing buffers to fear we construct buffers to our natural state of communion. Being buffered to our unity leaves us with nothing *but* our fear and our myriads of buffers to that fear. This "buffer world" of semantics chronically fails to insulate us from fear, anxiety, *or* death, but succeeds remarkably in insulating us from life.

7. Guilty!

Until Proven Dead

Most "training" of children depends on a wilful, specific employment of anxiety inducement. This consciously perpetrated crime is "guilting," an activity with which we are all involved throughout our lives.

Guilting is built on fear but requires some language development for its inception. Guilting can become fully operative only in a mind split from its primary process. The roots of self-doubt, on which guilting grows, are found in earliest anxiety.

No child could be guilted were his parents or "mothering-ones" not fear ridden. Anxiety, as fear without an object, is induced "unconsciously," but guilting is not. Guilting is induced very purposefully, though always cloaked under moral wraps. Guilting is employed by parents out of their own sense of guilt and anxiety, but always under the rationale that they are "training" their child.

Most parental "concerns" over their children generate from a fear of social censure. A child not supporting the cultural norms would reflect on the parents' own social image. The parent's own family is the strongest judge, and on a gradient come peer groups, neighbors, and then the larger abstractions, society, religion, and so on.

Even concerns over a child's possible physical injury orient toward fears of social condemnation for not "caring properly." Actual concern for the well being of the child takes second place. (As in public schools, where administrative fears of liability, public censure, school-board recriminations, taxpayer revolts, parental wrath, and so on, weigh heavier than concern for the child, and account for the bulk of the disciplinary regulations and general air of distrust and mutual resentment.) The pressure on parents to maintain a social image gives ample rationale for guilting under the wraps of "moral virtue." The classical example of the "Jewish mother" illustrates a tendency shared by all, and we recall Jesus's comment, "a man's worst enemies are those of his own household."

Newborns don't smile, but they learn to rapidly. Frowns, smiles, tones of voice, all link with anxiety, satisfaction of needs and survival. Judgment plays a dominant role long before any logical development begins. The infant survival system responds preverbally to a host of cues. The prelogical, preliterate modes of mind function outside language and "conscious" processes. Both infant and child pick up unexpressed negatives and fear.

As soon as there is any infant word play, the parent tends to shift to language-as-communication, long before the infant conceives of language in that sense. Most of the endless barrage of negatives resulting, the ceaseless "no-no's," register on the child as anxiety. Parental "reasoning" does not register on the prereasoning child. With the growing demand for verbal identification, the child is forced to focus less on primary modes of perceiving and more on verbal interactions. Language slowly enters as a grid intervening between data and response.

The child's resistance to abandoning his center brings on *verbal threats* of consequences for failure to comply. The child's threat-syndrome is then called into play semantically. At that point the child's physical identity, his placement of self in a world of real things, begins its slow shift to a social-semantic identity. His biological mechanisms for survival must start attending to verbal demands. An ambivalence enters, a division between inner balance and outward response to verbal stimuli.

A silent swat is worth a thousand words. Our organism is designed to learn by concrete interactions with reality. Animal mothers will bat their young about when necessary, and they learn forthwith. Nothing clears the air so quickly for a locked-in child as a single swift whack on the rear, just as nothing so confuses, fragments, and disturbs a child at the verbal barrage that passes for "reasoning," or threat.

Don Juan offered strange advice to Carlos concerning a "ruined" child. He recommended sudden, unexplained, and silent thrashings by a stranger every time the child behaved in an unacceptable manner.

Don Juan claimed that fright never hurt a child, but that nagging destroyed them.

Underlying much of our verbal assault on the young is a masochistic projection of our own frustration. Deep within we know that our words wound far more insidiously than anything else, and leave no outward mark. The "battered child syndrome" of current interest is a physical manifestation arousing our projected indignation. But the psychological equivalent is more prevalent. It just isn't immediately detectable. The *psychologically battered* child is observable only in the irrational behavior of each next generation.

Parental verbal threat is always unclear in intent to the child. The parents' own confusion, shifting focus, and muddy intent, create continual contradiction. The child lives in that underlying intent, too, an intent nearly always at variance with the surface "reasonings."

Threatening the child with future recriminations (this will be done to you and that will be done to you if you don't do *this* now) only furthers the flight-fight shift from physical reality to abstract verbal patterns.

The child's image of self has been described as threefold: good-me; bad-me; and not-me. The young child will often shift "blame" or the actions of "bad-me," over to an imaginary self, a "not-me," or an imaginary playmate. ("I didn't do it," our two-year-old Susan used to say. *"My Susie* did it." *My Susie* was her shadow-image designed to take the edge off our guilting.)

Through verbal play of "as-if" performances, the child attempts to manipulate the reactions of others and ward off guilting. Concealing through playacting that which might otherwise bring anxiety is a defensive step, but also the first step toward lying and an important element in the growing split of the psyche. As the child's outer compliance grows, his inner centeredness slowly transforms into a reflection on this semantic world of ambiguous and contradictory impingements. Sooner or later he must become what he beholds.

He reists being pulled off center, however, and this becomes the concern of educators. The child must be convinced of his insufficiency to deal with life, otherwise he will not pay attention to us parents, educators, preachers, policemen, politicians, doctors, lawyers, sergeants, billboards, Pentagons, undertakers.

Preliterate cultures depended on *willing imitation.* Imitation is play. The child was incorporated into the adult action-world through concrete action. Little language is needed for imitation. One "sees" and does. All children pick up most of their initial reality picture through imitative play. Imitation can only be of real events if it is to *lead* a child. Modern education must rely on motivation and the verbal since nonreality can't be imitated.

Childhood play should be apprenticeship to adult play. Only in the literate cultures have work and play been so categorized and split. Play is suspect in a literate culture based on a hostile universe and an incompleteness in life itself. A culture that can't play has no accommodation's for playful apprentices and must create a separate world for its young. Play is for playgrounds under careful supervision.

A smiling, laughing child is suspect in a school, for instance. He surely is, or intends being, naughty.

The drawn face, the slight, pensive frown, the serious-student look, quiet and attentive, is the paradigm, expressing prediction and control.

Language is as complicated an activity as the mind giving it birth. Yet the child grasps this inordinate complexity generally by his fourth year, and of his own volition. Most of the child's reality explorations are extensive and functional by his sixth year. And all this growth takes place spontaneously, through playful imitation and participation. A child knows joy in reality learning and seldom resists activity that is for his actual reality welfare. He is *programmed* to respond affirmatively to life. Play *is* his programmed response. Play is learning. The intellect grows by play. The highest forms of operational logic develop through play, and are short-circuited and thwarted by schooling.

Nothing we could do could force our children to do that which they naturally, spontaneously, and even joyously do within their first six years. Joy and spontaneity prove stronger than our anxiety inducements and guiltings, else the child would simply go autistic entirely.

Why is this situation of creative response so dramatically reversed after the sixth year? The child resists the negative and the irrational just as he rejected the anxiety nipple in the beginning. The child resists the fear and guilting involved in acculturation as he vigorously as he accepts early reality exploration and learning.

One summer I daily watched a tiny boy, not yet turned two, swimming with his older brothers. The little one would dive into the water with abandon and faith, in imitation of his paradigms. Occasionally he strangled, spat, sputtered, cried, regained his breath, and plunged again. He never exceeded his limits. He sensed his capabilities. No one ruined his spontaneous response to the water with fear talk. I am sure his paradigms in that (Mexican) family had all learned to swim in the same way and never gave it a thought.

Generally the parents' fear of social condemnation for "irresponsibility" is projected as "concern" for the child. Parents seldom distinguish between their own general state of anxiety and a concern for their children's actual well-being.

This has led us, in our strangely abstracted illusions, to an extreme overprotection of children that has hilarious results. Television is surrendered to so unanimously because of its safe and stable placement of children for long hours. On every hand our society sets up buffers between the child and reality, lest that child be "hurt." (Never mind what TV does to that psyche, the body is safe and so one's image-as-parent is safe.) Every aspect of the child's life is *supervised* in one way or another as a security device. Dangers are systematically eliminated. One isn't allowed fireworks any more, but goes to the stadium to watch a fireworks display. (I am not championing fireworks, the example is simply very much apropos.)

Buffering the child against danger throughout his formative years, we then, somewhere around his sixteenth year, put him behind the wheel of two or three hundred horsepower, turn him loose on the freeways, and wonder why the vast majority of automobile accidents occur with young drivers.

Don Juan points out that the "body likes danger." The "body likes to be frightened." Anyone with children knows that children love to be play-frightened in "let's pretends" with safe parents. Children play at fright all the time. Young people decisively need to confront danger and seek it in anticultural counterfeits.

Specific fear-with-an-object can serve as an enormous relief valve for our homeostatic forces overworked by anxiety and the constant maneuvering of death avoidance. Witness the strange doomsday exhilaration of wartime; the attraction of horror movies; the panderings of television; the holiday malevolence of public hangings in our recent past; the avid, nonrational, riot-tinged push to witness fire, disaster, tragedy, wreck. The more insular our bufferings to life, the more extreme our vicarious indulgences in violence and death.

We are taught to believe that only through the constant alert watchfulness of the trained intellect can the inadequate hostile life-forces be kept in check. Trust in natural processes is unknown in the acculturated, just as it was natural and unquestioned in the child's early explorations. We first caution a child about the dangers of water and of his inability to survive in it. To make sure he heeds our warnings we play on his fear and anxiety. We give him a target to fear. Then we might prepare to *teach* him how to swim. By the time our preparatory ventures are over, he will be locked in a knot of fear that will need all our training techniques to undo.

The learning he then must undergo is channeled through verbal instructions, incessant commands, a sea of verbage drowning him if the water doesn't. The response which could have been a joyous, simple one of discovery-imitation becomes a series of clumsy, stiff battles of muscle against muscle, response against response, until finally the body can take over that which it could have done in the beginning.

Motivation is of great concern to educators. Motivation is thought of as a kind of internal machine that once set in motion might drive the child to do what is desired of him. Motivation works only indirectly. If the child does as desired it is generally only to avoid the guilting of those trying to "motivate" him.

Education is formalized acculturation. The seeds of our current madness are liberally planted in the schoolroom, flower in the university, and reseed over the land. Most children dislike school, though they feel guilty about it. This attitude is mirrored back and forth between teacher and student. Only threats, reprisals, recriminations keep the lid on.

Kindergartners love school. It is a form of play. The first grader goes along with the game. It was fun the first year. By the second grade things have started souring. By the fourth grade the jig is up. By junior high school all hell breaks loose. High school is quieter only because of the apathy setting in after the abortive, futile outbreak of junior high. An uneasy truce then exists between teachers and students to ride this thing out with a minimum of trouble to all concerned.

The "as-if" performance takes on new twists in the student-teacher battles for survival. A strange sense of fair play often surfaces. A visitor will bring the children rallying to the teacher's defense by putting up a good front. They know intuitively that the teacher is as much a victim as they are. When scrutinized by the public eye there is an unspoken gesture to play as-if, and bail the teacher out.

Everyone on the "outside" knows what really goes on in school, for all went through it. Everyone simply pretends not to know once they are free of it. Or they practice selective blindness for their own sanity, knowing the situation to be both intolerable and irremediable.

Or, having suffered themselves, some adults feel that such suffering must, therefore, be "good for them," making a virtue of necessity rather as the legionnaire's snarling, drunken glee over the "young hippies" getting sent over to Vietnam—"make men of 'em" (should they survive).

More often is the sad double-think hope of so many parents that somehow, *this* time, with *their* children, the machine might not make hamburger of those children, even though the parents know it is a hamburger machine.

School is the most clear-cut, embarrassingly naked example of the acculturation process at its best. The more unsure the whole procedure, the more muddy its intent, the greater grows the administrative cry for more of everything—more money, buildings, teachers, administrators, counselors. The bankruptcy of the whole bureaucracy would become apparent were "blame" not tossed out in every direction.

As Arthur Ceppos said of most education: "It is an endless preparation for something that never takes place."

Yet, in spite of "more of everything" the morass simply grows heavier and more impossible. A generation of householders has virtually bankrupted itself in response to the bankrupt cries of education, to no avail. The outpouring of money for lavish physical plants has been like upholstering an electric chair. The victims still resent the end result.

Inauthenticity and inadequacy are the constant accusations from the school and reverberated in the home. Consider the recent rash of billboards put out by the educational association devoted to the horrors of being a high school dropout.

On every hand we are threatened, as is the student, with every kind of reprisal. We are even threatened for not believing we are in a bad way and working madly to amend some "failing." We are easy to intimidate since in our deep knowing we are aware that we are fragmented and off balance. Having no specific reason for this anxiety, cultural guilting easily finds roots to feed our disease.

We have no way of articulating our anxiety. Acculturation convinces us that our "condition" is due to our personal failure to comply properly with the culture. The success of our culture is dependent on convincing us that there is no split of mind at all—but rather that we have only failed to acquire the proper "bridges" to wholeness offered by the cultural system. Or, equally effective, those bridges need repair and updating, jobs which only our life investment can attend.

There could be no swimming teacher were all children initiated into the water as the young child at our pool. For a successful swimming teacher you must first have a pupil, one convinced of his natural lack. The age of the professional rests on producing the incompetent.

The inducement of fear never ceases. As adults we are just getting into the full swing of it. We both inflict and suffer guilt and anxiety on an ever wider basis. All of us are daily accused by every billboard, advertisement, newscast, authority pronouncement, Pentagon alarm, political warcry, or recent horror from the imaginative laboratories of the American Medical Association. We are ignorant, inadequate, unworthy, unnecessary, unloveable, unacceptable, vulnerable to the plunder of the opposition party, vulnerable to the ravages of endless disease, subject to the horrors of hell on death, and we smell bad.

All the needed correctives can be had, of course, by our proper response to the cultural priests dispensing the commodities of salvation. Or, if none of this suffices our particular bent of mind, then we should cook up some healing salves of our own to peddle and not stand around complaining.

The great accusers: governments, businesses, Pentagons, CIA's, churches, schools, jails have always been with us in some guise, and may always be. These things *are* culture and they are self-perpetuating. For every young person trying to "drop out," a dozen thoroughly programmed, well-acculturated students quietly go ahead training to sustain the system. The dropout makes news, but he makes no changes and he has nowhere to go.

Though they change vestments with ease, the cultural priests have never changed functionally, nor can they. Our contemporary culture is maintained, however, by convincing you that you *can* change things. Our culture convinces you that you can "throw out the rascals in Washington," or wherever, or the robber barons or the egghead liberals, and by your energy help redress the wrongs. Our culture survives by keeping you filled with the *hope for change* and the notion that everything *can be* changed.

A person is considered "normal" or properly acculturated when fear and guilt are his norm, and buffers to such "natural conditions" are his life pursuit. Most people who fault culture are convinced that great remedial changes are in the offing. This always means better buffers for all. These activities leave the central issue carefully untouched and spin the merry-go-round even faster.

That we are left only with our intellect as "protection" against a hostile cosmos, and that our intellect is a semantic creation, with semantics subordinate and supportive of the cultural process, brings us full circle.

This circular definition of reality can be summed up as the death concept. Every accusation of guilt is a threat of death in some guise: death of one's self-image; hopes of fulfillment; sexual prowess; attractiveness; security; ease; comfort; health and on it goes. Literal death is threatened indirectly. The war makers threaten death at the hands of the current enemy unless we properly prime the death machines with our energies and money; the disease makers threaten, in fact guarantee, death from every latest death fad, should the counteractions not be sought (regardless of staggering cost), the lawmakers promise more penalties and stuff the overstuffed prisons; the scientists assure us of death, not just of our life but of all life. If the big bang must be abandoned, there is the New Black Hole. Or as a last resort, though dull, there is always the second law of thermodynamics to fall back on, to get everything and everybody in the end. Insurance companies remind us of our death in the form of the worse fate for those left behind—should we fail to apportion those companics their fair share of our energies and toil. The preachers remind us of our death and the fate of our elusive souls should we be the spiritual equivalents of high-school dropouts.

Yet death is strangely taboo. Even as there is no greater current guilting than *not* sending your "loved one" to the death factory to be drugged into their personal oblivion, doctors will have little to do with death. Such is for nurses and orderlies and the machinery of the "intensive care ward," (probably the most macabre device of all twentieth-century nightmares.) And all of us *willingly give over* our responsibilities and surrender to the death profession, lest we should have actually to feel, touch, see death itself. We give in to guilting and allow no one the right and dignity of dying their own death. To enter consciously into that last great adventure has become anathema.

The drugged dispensing is followed by a final obscenity, the undertaker and his "embalming." "We make them look so real," one ad ran, in the odd pretense that it hasn't really happened. And then the "everlasting plot of ground" marked with marble memorial–"show that you *really care.*" "Memories are all you have now, you know."

Guilting focuses all attention on the cultural context, and leaves no place to hide. Guilting brings on judgment of neighbor against neighbor, family member against member, government against government—each dispensing equal executioners periodically to uphold their just decrees, and so on throughout the whole globe.

Culture requires an inordinate amount of energy to maintain itself. (Don Juan claimed that the cultivation of well-being required no more energy than the maintenance of our dis-ease.) Culture is the most jealous of gods. Fear and isolation are held as our natural state, inflicted on us by a hostile universe. "You can't change human nature," the Naked Ape proponents chime. Contexts can be changed, however, and all energy must be expended toward that end. Any move toward centering is suspect.

Every breakdown in our buffers to despair is an

opportunity for embracing that despair. To be in despair is to be *without hope.* Don Juan and Jesus live *without hope.* Hope is futuristic. The whole man lives in the eternal moment of now, and needs nothing more. Psychiatry, like religion, is designed to reinstate one's buffers should they collapse. Psychiatry is the priest standing at the door allowing no one entry to the Kingdom. The Psychiatrist *mediates for one* until one's mediation devices can be restored. Psychiatry, as religion, buffers against despair. (Ronald Laing caught a glimmering of this, but apparently, as did Luther, drew back from the awesomeness of the implications.)

Culture is hope. Hope keeps one contextually oriented. Any move toward centering is suspect, since only the eccentric man, off balance and outside himself, is predictable and controllable. Nothing so upsets the bishop as the rumor of a saint in his parish.

8. Will to Power

"What will you be when you grow up?" is a prime cultural "guilter." The fantasy response of childhood grows into a survival issue in adolescence. Refusal to accept and respond to this question brings on threats of lifetime recriminations.

The question implies that whatever one is, a child,

preadolescent, or adolescent, he is in an incomplete, temporary stage, of significance only as it points ahead. The question denies the moment and focuses on a future. Further, the question implies that without the pursuit-to-become something, (such as one of the myriad adult-images offered by culture,) one will *have* no being. Indeed, it implies that one *has* no being. Being, it seems, must be attained.[1]

This question as accusation happens to the child at about the same age in all cultures. The question, implying inauthenticity of one's present state, links with the loss of self to the persona mask occurring in adolescence. The young person is easily guilted by the question "What will you be?" since he is unsure of what he is. (He may have been told in Sunday School that he is a "child of God," but this notion, dropped in a brief hour once a week, is overwhelmingly denied by the whole social fabric the rest of the week.)

The question falls on fertile soil and plays on a rich network of fear and anxiety. Identity is *withheld* by the question. Granting the young person a stable place is held out in front of him as a carrot before the donkey.

Persuading him to accept the inauthenticity of his natural state, and move from centeredness to the peripheries of a social-semantic has been the job of education to this point. Education's task then becomes persuading the young person to choose an image of what he might become, from those images currently needed by the society. Then education "prepares" him to *pursue* that image. The first quarter to one third of one's life is devoted to preparing for one's chosen illusion.

This image pursuit fulfills the earlier persona mask,

which has been secret if conscious at all. The chance is given to convert this covert energy into an overt performance granted sanction by society.

Archaic cultures had a ready-made choice and a ritualized mode for becoming the clearly defined cultural image. The codified procedures of the rites-of-passage kept the cyclic culture intact and assured prediction and control. One served a stylized preset culture with stylized, preset acts. A minimum of ambiguity or variation, as well as a minimum of anxiety concerning one's "identity," existed.

As the mask effect of the social ego takes over the child of our culture, his "identity" shifts to a semantic context. Homeostasis must find stable placement in a semantic reality. The authentic is that which offers cultural sanction and the drive for personal authenticity is a drive for ego-image verification by other people. This drive continues usually into the mid-thirties at least. By then, success or failure in becoming one's mask and winning authenticity is usually played out.

The child is "ego centered" without being "selfish." His world simply generates from him and is complete. The child doesn't have to become anything. He already is. The question "What will you be?" can only be formulated by a split-mind culture and can only be inflicted on a mind finally split. By being denied identity until such hypothetical time as one shall win "self-verification," one's life energy must give over to the culture.

Our culture, in distinction from more archaic ones, offers a rich variety of personal-image projections for pursuit. These change according to the needs of a flexible culture. The more gifted are offered "careers" on a graded scale of salvation. These avenues of pursuit *are* culture. The drive for such attainments is the life of the culture.

The pursuit of adult verification links with the earlier buffer shield. The life investment of self, energy, time, attention, and hope of fulfillment creates a buffer effect. Such activity is the only real "insulator" against despair. The hope of attainment keeps one's energies focused and staves off a confrontation with the split of mind.

Heretofore the bulk of this guilt procedure fell on the males of our culture. Female authenticity was more concrete and almost assured. A pseudo-rite of passage for females sufficed until most recently and still holds in conservative areas. Highly romanticized and ritualized, this rite had three clearly defined steps: 1) engagement–stamp of authentic desirability: 2) marriage–authentic femininity: 3) motherhood–final sanction with archetypal fertility status.

Actual arrival was largely automatic for most women, as it was and is almost automatically impossible for men. The procedure produced its own anxiety for women, however, since failure in this domain left few avenues open. And in a world where females outnumber males, particularly after the periodic and regular cyclic round of wars, an underlying frustration has existed. Increasingly, the sanctioned state of motherhood itself has been found dust and ashes too, cloaked by sentiment as it may be. The bitter status of women has been evident throughout all the cultures, from Aborigine on down.

Perhaps as a result of "universal education" and "intellectual achievement," the female was inadvertently hooked into the same inauthenticity accusations as the male. (No more simple home economics and maybe some shorthand and typing: science, technology, and math are for everyone.) Thus the necessary authenticity-pursuit syndrome being induced into the male hooked the female as well.

This has had disruptive effects, typical of the often hilarious irrationalities of culture. We see the feminine-liberation movement reject a fairly stable image-authenticity procedure for the extremely heartbreaking illusion crippling the male.

The search for image verification implements and complements the cultural grid of data screening. The data for verification of one's image of self must come from the cultural context, from consensus. The "other person" and the whole social context is always seen through a grid of apparent survival needs. Each of us, functioning in this way, is the actual drive for prediction and control as we strive to attain and maintain our culturally created image.

Image verification operates on two levels: the long-range goals of "career" or life investment, and the immediate short-term needs for immediate-context image feedback. Homeostasis still drives for stable placement of self, and can never relax, since the semantic context consists only of ego centers each trying to achieve identity or stable placement.

We demand self-verification from those important to us—which means those we think might fill our verification need. We try to maneuver this "other" into compliance with our grid. This "other," of course, has the same grid functioning driving him. Grids function identically, though each is unique to the individual's experience. So, grid needs vary and human relations are made of continual clashes of survival needs. Each subtly tries to outmaneuver the other and gain compliance.

Should two grids coincide on a sufficient number of need points (which generally means that two people find their as-if performances complementary), a "happy" relation may result—even marriage. Positive feedback is simultaneously given both. Positive feedback changes grid needs, however, and diminishes the need for and will finally dispose of that kind of grid. Sooner or later, as a result, each of us "fails the other" in this world of images. And, each of us senses these failures to be a breakdown in our insulation against despair. We then "suffer a depression." (Antidepressants are the chemical rage among the cultural priests.)

Depression is disappointment of a predicted goal, and all goals are buffers to despair. Everyone knows chronic depressions on a wide scale, since goal prediction, attainment, and then collapse, or, nonattainment and *shift* of goal, is the modus operandi of culture. Either way lies "depression." When depression threatens a total rupture of one's buffers to despair, depression becomes a serious medical concern. For annihilation of one's buffers to despair is annihilation of one's cultural orientation. So avoidance of depression is achieved by the continual buffering of our insulators. This leads to the active, indeed, increasingly hyperactive busyness that we call "progress."

The cultural process produces a split and then offers the ameliorative. The ameliorative can never be attained since the entire affair exists in the imagination of a split mind. The products of depression cannot alleviate depression any more than gravity can do other than its own thing. All pursuits and all grids move for a wholeness that lies outside such pursuits. Positive feedback attainments never alleviate the underlying need, so new pursuits or grids must be adopted.

A kind of pseudoverification by a process of default or elimination often occurs. After the young person has played his hand, rushing out on the "stage of life," clamoring for attention and verification for his image act, and if need be, shifting from image to image, he will often collapse inwardly into quiet resignation. He docilely sinks into the nearest niche of least resistance and quits. At that point the cultural sifting process will have attained its quota of "winners" and the amorphous mass of losers, necessary to sustain the system, are then accorded a kind of booby prize. One's social context (predominantly one's family) then may reward the loser with "Ah. At last he has *found* himself, and settled down." Down it is indeed. This often occurs in the mid-thirties, a time when a peculiar tendency for heavy, compulsive drinking has been noted.

9. Ace up the Sleeve

Hope

Our culture survives by the continual development of buffers to our despair. Buffers to despair also serve the pursuits for authenticity in our will-to-power.

Over a period of time we forget the buffer effect of our childhood persona mask and try to become that mask. With adolescence, orientation shifts to social context, and our inner identity is lost. Then guilting has a free reign over our rich background of anxiety, and the question "what will you be?" takes on serious dimensions.

The young adolescent carries within him a nameless nostalgia, a sense of loss that is inarticulate, ignored by his society, and nursed privately within. His only connection left for escape from isolation seems through language and culture.

If the adolescent's parents sense that he is mirroring their own folly, their hopes of vicarious atonement through their children are thwarted. Conversely, if they sense that he is not aping their graces, they find their static world view threatened. Either way, the young have a hard time.

Nevertheless, along with paradigms for life-investment goals, a raft of temporary paradigms are given, from movies, television, advertisements, successful peers and superiors. These demonstrate a set of postures, stances, and gestures by which the young may cloak their lack of identity. This cloak acts as a mask of acceptability while one trains to become one's true "image," the one chosen in response to "what will you be?"

Acting out current paradigms furthers the transference to social context. Our poses and gestures become our body's identity check or "reality check." One of the reasons sensory isolation is frightful is that the body can't check and reinforce its identity by such methods. In the movie theater, for instance, should the projector break down and the audience be stranded for any time in a dark silence, immediately a shuffling, coughing, rustling movement begins, as each person initiates body movements and noises for close-quarter sensory checks on reality beingness. Suddenly denied their vicarious reality, feedback for their "long-range sensors" of sight and sound, close-quarter, tactile senses are brought into play.

Early adolescence was the period for archaic rites-of-passage into the adult world. The church copied this in its ineffectual rite-of-confirmation, which was meant to incorporate the young person into the Body of Christ.

The young of today have no rites other than spontaneous creations by their peer groups: driver's license (which carries some social recognition of arrival), cigarettes, and sex. The best the adult world can do is capitalize on this "subculture" commercially, or use it for guilting. (Schooling is our substitution for the rites-of-passage. This is the substituting of a concrete reality-confrontation with a semantic abstraction. The rite-of-passage was quick and effective. Schooling grows longer and longer and less effective as its abstractions grow more obtuse and vague.)

Culture-as-guilting must keep an unsureness in the young, otherwise motivation to accept acculturation would break down. To gain authenticity as a real, by-god person, one must win feedback through the culturally approved feedback channels.

Since one's adult reality is determined by social context, all drives center, sooner or later, on the attempt to *realign* that context, or align one's self more smoothly within it. Prediction and control remain cultural by becoming personal.

Our personality image must complement our cultural pattern to be successful. Verification of ego image is only possible through other people and established cultural procedures. This leads to what don Juan called "pimping" for others; living one's life in compliance with and for the gratification of others. The acculturated person acts out a life as he thinks a nebulous set of expectancies dictates.

There are two obvious ways for winning feedback: through gaining authenticity for one's adopted image; and through acquisition of culturally desirable things. Material possession and social image are almost always complementary if not synonymous. Those material things considered desirable shift and change continually, always offering new pursuits. Such pursuit is itself an insulation against despair.

To be successful within our current system is successfully to acquire buffers; or, better, to seize control of a buffer system; or best, originate a new form of buffer–which is hailed as progress or revelation.

The billboard threatened the young person against dropping out lest he be denied *beingness* all his life. A new one warned that one would never have *things* should one drop out. A new billboard then even threatened that one would be denied a *name*: "BOY!" the ad ran. "That's all they'll ever call *you* if you don't . . ."

Possession of cultural buffers is possession of *beingness*. The unknown tramp found dead under the bridge (it could be a don Juan) merits scant attention. The rich man found dead in his mansion is a sensation.

To lack "things" is to lack identity. Underlying the passion of "backward nations" for industrialization is the implied accusation of inauthenticity by the "having-nations." Thus we export our madness.

The Vietnamese village was wiped out without too serious a concern–just grass shacks and gooks grubbing in the dirt. One doesn't cling to life, but to things.

Buffers are effective only as entertainments of mind, staving off the confrontation with the split self. So the winning of personal buffers always fails to insulate for long. The real need is within and the projection onto out-there only prolongs the alienation. So new buffers must be continually developed.

Since, to the bright ones, the only real authenticity is gaining control of and expanding buffer systems or originating new ones, a continual attack against established buffer systems is part of the scene. This poses as "bold new attacks" on our decadent, outworn culture. Actually it is the only way for culture to renew itself. Nothing changes culture's function.

The will-to-power seeks, and creates by its seeking, the buffer system. One can "elect" his choice of image and pursuit of fulfillment. The boy of simple background can attain to the White House, or opt for motorcycle, leather jacket, and attached girl behind. Don Juan's nephew needed only a motorcycle for his authenticity grant.

"If I had a million, then everything would be OK" is an unsophisticated but effective form of this complex. The pursuit acts as entertainment of mind staving off despair. When the pursuit finally crashes in ruins, or when the pursuit is overwhelmingly successful, the buffer effect is no longer operable, and one has no insulation against his despair. (Thus the utter nastiness of some really rich people.) Only in the pursuit of, or the first flushed excitement of possession of, a buffer, does the insulation effect work.

An effective part of the system comes from those with too much acumen for plain buffer pursuit. Some realize that the culture is itself at fault. A culture is no more than a buffer system to its own induced fear, so the buffer system is obviously inadequate, in need of repair or replacement. This stimulates that individual with too much intellect or talent for straight rabbit-chasing down the track to devote his life to building more comfortable tracks and more attractive rabbits. Thus the best minds and energies are channeled into service of the culture.

A church marquis, one of those glass cases out front announcing next Sunday's attractions, carried this stunning guilting buffer:

"Be Ashamed To Die, Until You Have Won Some Victory For Mankind."

The actual attainment of such "victories" may prove disillusioning, but new illusions are always forthcoming.

For the unimaginative this means the pursuit of new things, the installment merry-go-round of obsolescence. To the more imaginative who need ego verification, buffer failure is attributed to some missing piece yet to be attained. Goal obsolescence immediately establishes a new goal that "really has it." This perpetuation device works on all levels, in all institutions.

This proves as true in our so-called "new-spirituality" as in the grossest of old materiality. Culturally there is no difference in these apparently opposite functions. Culture is strengthened by either, so long as pursuit and hope are involved.

The church disintegrates as a buffer system, and hordes of eager replacements scrabble to fill the vacuum. Last year's drug scene fades to biofeedback feeding alpha waves to mind-control prophets riding the circuit with acupuncturists and high-energy mental-states-through-protein-intake-boys making way for electronic human biocomputed data-feeding mind-zapping behind the Iron Curtain secrets of ESP, black magic, ooh-ah chemistry-clowns with astral travel and god-in-the pill, the test tube, the sleep-learning machine, and LSD in the cosmic tank while the Swami-of-the-Month-Club jets this year's Savior fresh from India–younger and fresher than ever, the kids have the spending money these days–expanding awareness, expanding the new-consciousness, expanding the lungs in hyperventilated bio-energetic ozone sniffing in the Himalayas, sensory-overloading the witches-cradled Egyptian Mamma-cat Cleopatra's Altered States of Consciousness in a more-More concupiscent-cavitied infinitely-capacitated craving-craw crunching up this whole goddamned cosmos–Oh my God Yes–they missed with that Tower of Babel because they were ignorant hicks–we've got Technology. We'll put this thing together right and take that Kingdom of Heaven by storm.

After each go-round, when the dust settles, it appears that something was missing. Here we are, just about the same–a bit low on adrenalin (that *was* an exciting seminar-workshop weekend!) but we're just as split, alienated, afraid. But wait–dig the latest from Calcutta, and off we go–to the newest psychic-fix parley, the Chatauqua Circuit risen from the dead.

The ace-up-the-sleeve syndrome can never be exhausted. The housewife shopping for trinkets, stuffing her overstuffed house with more junk, envying her neighbor's larger house and greater piles of junk; nagging her husband to "buy up" in the world and get out of this dump; stuffing her overstuffed body with junk; stifling her long-denied sex with junk and eyeing her daughter's slim with jaundiced eye; and eyeing the telly for laughs only to eye the new round of trinkets and junk–itching her up for the next day's scratch to fill the void, one more cycle in staving off despair.

The young man no longer so young still pursuing the gimmickry and trickery of his teens and twenties, illusions of becoming his image shattered beyond repair; knowing of no way of being but being those postures, stances, and gestures trained to attain the unattainable; the resorting to alcohol in those mid-thirties; slipping into that aching, maddening, heart-breaking nostalgia of the late-Lolita thirties and early forties with their mystically desperate longing for very young girls–the last flickering memory of that long-ago innocence lost, before the thread of life was broken–and then the long slow slide into the paunch, the slack jaw, the glassy eye of belligerent lost hope.

Still, to the end, all respond on cue. All are predictable and controllable, as all keep playing that one last ace-up-the-sleeve. And it is this ace that blocks each from cycling out of illusion into what should be their real maturity, an abandonment of image making and a move toward reunion of that split self.

Only those who realize, somewhere along the game, that *no* ace-up-the-sleeve can heal one's split; that there *are* no amelioratives, no techniques, no systems; that one is always bankrupt in that mad competition in which no one ever wins; that one is truly poor with nowhere to go and nothing to do—only those few might wake from sleep.

10. Roof-Brain Chatter

The Mature Mind

Roof-brain chatter is a term I picked up from reading Robert de Ropp. Others call the activity our "stream of consciousness."[1] Joyce used the phenomena as a literary device. Tracing the origins of this "'internal speech" performance gives a short summary of acculturation.

Recall how our body-threat reaction to a physical

world has been tranferred to an ego-image threat in a semantic one. The tiger is no longer much of a threat around that next bush, but there is mother-in-law, spouse, children, boss, parents, red-necks, blacks, dollars, Republicans, Russians, the vagaries of sexual athletics, and so on.

The flight-fight system, only occasionally called on in a tiger world, is never at rest in our semantic one. (Not even in sleep—one dreams of being caught in Times Square with no clothes on.) The homeostatic stabilizers are overtaxed in our semantic sea, yet never get the ship on even keel. As homeostasis and the threat syndrome are converted to culture, and the acculturated mind to its semantic universe, semantic feedback from others becomes the stuff of life and reality. Authenticity of self and world becomes a matter of words.

A child will talk to himself out loud and unconcerned. He verbalizes his exploration of reality. Talking-out his world is his address to the objects named, self included. Under pressure of conformity to use language only as communication with other people, this talking out of his world gets internalized. (Aspects of his growing operational thinking may be involved in this internalization as well, but social forces predominate.) Schooling clinches the defensive maneuver of internalization.

Internal talk "joins forces" with the "real-me" operating behind the outer mask of social compliance. As the demands from out-there become increasingly insistent on the child, the "in-here" of the real-me must attend more and more to that activity impinging. Finally, internal talk becomes only a reflection of the outer pose.

Talking to one's self inside one's head acts in a

homeostatic manner. Through it we try to achieve a pseudo-stable-sameness of the semantic reality. A semantic reality must have a steady source of words. Talk is compulsive on every hand. And print is almost hypnotic in its pull on the literate-conditioned mind. We are hardly in McLuhan's "post-literate world" as yet. Billboards function as "reality checks." Language activity becomes a survival necessity and roof-brain chatter forms a stable semantic background continually reinforcing the social world.

By maturity the practice of internal speech is virtually nonstop. It probably continues unabated even in sleep. Some dreams may well be forms of roof-brain chatter. Without the modifying reality checks of other people and other things, this night form gets bizzarre, as in sensory isolation.

Personal awareness is largely this stream of roof-brain talk. Even when actual feedback from another source is coming in, roof-brain chatter goes right ahead, prestructuring, tape-looping, resenting, planning one's rebuttal, fogging inputs and creating static. Listening to one's actual social world, much less a "natural world," is difficult for the acculturated mind, while the various subtle body-knowing processes stand no chance of being perceived.

Roof-brain chatter can be categorized into three states, past, present, and future, or guilt and resentment, hostility, and anxiety.

The past event carried over in roof-brain chatter centers around resentment and guilt. Good-time memories are played over too, elaborated into rich fantasies stripped of all negatives. Guilt and resentment involve fear, however, and get the bulk of attention. These "threats" are never direct body-threats, of course, though they may finally be fed into the memory bank of the body in some way. Resentment and guilt are generally threats to one's cultural image of self.

Resentment is hardly an incidental slight within the playback system. It is deadly serious and the source of many bodily ills. The mind tape-loops (John Lilly's term) a bad event, fires it into play over and over, lining up the sequences in new, winning ways. Image verification unwinds the movies in the head the way it *should* have been: (. . . "take *that* you . . ." ". . . and I should have said to him I says . . ." "why didn't I just go ahead and . . ."—at which point one does just that, one "goes ahead" over and over in roof-brain imaginings).

The whole body often mobilizes according to these fantasy plays. Muscles tighten, blood rushes about, adrenaline is produced, and all the stuff generates for fighting, arguing, mating, or whatever is going on in the head. For roof-brain chatter reverses the body's natural response system. Rather than informing the ego intellect of one's ambient situation, the body-knowing processes are informed by the roof-brain. And to the body system, adjusted to internally produced symbols from the earliest object-constancy period on, information is information.

Our resentment grid screens the present moment for similarities to past slights. We replay recent events for similarities with long-standing slurs. The body system, designed to handle actual dangers, operates in a similar way, but below awareness. Converted to this roof-brain reflection, the system runs out-of-phase, in reverse gear. It is kicked into continuous motion by word triggers from every direction.

Good feedback also acts as an effective grid screening out the present moment. Good memories lead to the attempt to duplicate such events by manipulating current cues, as rehearsed ad nauseum in roof-brain prestructurings.

Either way, positive or negative, reflective memory tangles future expectancies onto past recollections and projects the resulting mess onto the present moment, neatly canceling whatever opportunity a *now* might actually offer.

Roof-brain chatter acts as a pseudohomeostatic system. We furnish ourselves a stable optimum feedback world of ego-image verification. The present moment, what little might filter through the grid of resentment is fogged by latent hostility. Hostility toward the present results from real or imagined similarities with past bad times, or the possibilities of such reproduction. We redress past wrongs in tape-looped correction and project such prestructuring onto current data.

The present carries the seed of potential hostility, and our intellect attempts to manipulate the current event to give a predictable future. We further check the present for proper response to our gestures, stances, and postures played for image verification. The responses we desire from the present are never forthcoming. The infinite contingencies of reality never seem to match our grids. So new resentment material is always close at hand.

Future evaluation states revolve around high-feedback fantasy (the Walter Mitty syndrome) and around the What-If syndrome (What-If the sun should go out? Who has the flashlight? Insurance companies get fat off this one). Anxiety concerning the "future" revolves around security in general, the body and its health, ego images, possessions, attachments, loved ones, position, career, and so on.

This stew of resentment, hostility, and anxiety is

never clear cut in the roof-brain. Few ideas ever play themselves out in that kaleidoscopic montage. *Crack* readers will recall my outlining how all great creative "Eureka!" discoveries break through at odd moments when, among other things, this broken record effect of the roof-brain dims.

Roof-brain chatter makes up the bulk of one's "mental life." This activity filters out the present moment, drowns the primary perceptions in sheer head noise, and grounds one in a stasis of imaginary chaos. An American Indian said the white man was deafened by his own tongue. That Indian would have been astonished could he have tuned in on that internal chatter. An ancient Hebrew said: "Be still and know that I am God." Roof-brain chatter has been around for a long time.

For the acculturated mind there *is* no present moment. Our past was not the events tape-looped as "memory," and the merry-go-round of future imaginings never comes about. Perception, the door to life in this moment, is warped into a sharply curtailed process. The acculturated man lives, as the Buddhist claimed, in a world of illusion.

This body lock-up effect of tying in the homeostatic threat syndrome with the semantic universe of culture is impossible to dislodge. Consider the tenacity of your "roof-brain chatter" alone. It stands as the stumbling block to virtually every "system" setting out to "free one," or enlarge one's consciousness. And roof-brain chatter has its social counterpart in the "world." Our internal chatter is only a personalized form of a far more stringent and persuasive verbal force operating throughout the globe. Culture seems greater than the sum of its parts.

Yet, the infinite capacity for rationalization, assured by acculturation, and the natural cocreative capacity of the mind, can "mock-up" subjective simulations for almost any desired effect without in any way disturbing the homeostatic-cultural interlock. We can shift or alter our *mediants* between sense and percept and obtain novel results without disturbing our cultural response. The cultural organism doesn't need verbal agreement; indeed, the most strident voices raised against culture serve it just as faithfully as any politician. The underlying function is what counts, and on our functional response, so thoroughly conditioned by culture, our culture can always count.

If I seem to have overdrawn my picture in the first half of this study, I invite you to look again at the results of acculturation: examine the *quality* of life, the well-being of your own self, or the lack of it; read a newspaper; look at television; listen to an average person tell how things "really are" with him; note the millions of amphetamine-barbituates legally prescribed (such are the mysteries of law) and dispensed to keep souls who can no longer stand *anything* in a gray void where nothing happens; the four gallons of alcohol consumed per capita per year; the mess of "illegal" drugs drawing wildly mad sentences from alcoholic judges; look into the medical world, the hospitals and psychiatric wards; the overstuffed prisons; the chaos of your local schools; life in the cities; that marvelous circus, Our Capitol, Washington, D.C.

I haven't so much tried to overdraw the picture as to strip away hope—the eternal ace-up-the-sleeve by which one's desire to be whole is always led back into the tight circular fears of acculturation.

Only the stripped-down mind, one recognizing the

full extent of the poverty of our split state, could ever come close to giving up allegiance, without rationalization, to the perpetual promises of culture. Only the bankrupt soul can open the mind.

Part Two

Interlude

Susanne Langer believed that language arose from singing–from outbursts of ecstasy. Language, she insisted, was not an economic invention; it did not arise from "adaptation," it was not a survival maneuver.

In Thailand, the biologist C. R. Carpenter studied a species of gibbons that sang.[1] Carpenter found a cave in a cliffside overlooking one of the huge trees in which a tribe of these long-armed, manlike apes lived. There he set up recording and photography equipment, often only thirty feet from the creatures.

These strong-voiced gibbons have numerous musical calls heard throughout the day, but their morning "unison chorus," beginning each day, fills the whole forest. At daybreak the gibbons climb from their nesting places in the lower branches and gather in the topmost parts of the tree. There they begin singing on the same pitch, an E on our scale. Periodically and with precision they shift up one half step at a time, each half-step rise preceded by the original E as a grace note.

As they grow higher on the scale so does the rising sun, and the song increases in a steady crescendo. Finally the tribe reaches the octave above their starting note, and there they enter into a full-throated trill, at which point their bodies quiver in what appears an ecstasy. Then the trill subsides, a hush falls over the forest, and the tribe remains silent before quietly descending from the tree and going about their other rituals of the day.

Let me repeat a little quatrain from William Blake, which I used in *Crack*:

> How do you know but every bird
> that wings the airy way,
> Is an enormous world of delight,
> Closed to your senses five?

Cassirer, one of Susanne Langer's teachers, considered language to be bound with mythmaking—spontaneous expressions of the great dramas of life, the earth, the sky, the succession of day and night, the seasons, storms, the tides. According to Cassirer, language grew from responses called forth by numinous participation in cosmic acts. Ecstatic outbursts were called forth by overwhelming events and were later recalled as denotative of that event. Symbol formation is always stimulus substitution for concrete events, and mythic symbols grew as expressions standing for divine manifestations. Language ensued.

Orpingalik, the Eskimo, said: "Songs are thoughts, sung out with the breath when people are moved by great forces and ordinary speech no longer suffices. Man is moved just like the ice floe sailing here and there out in the current. His thoughts are driven by a flowing force when he feels joy, when he feels sorrow. Thoughts can wash over him like a flood, making his blood come in gasps and his heart throb . . . it will happen that the words we need will come of themselves. When the words we want to use shoot up of themselves—we get a new song."[2]

The Zen Master speaks of "It" breathing one. Inhalation, pneuma, inspiration, prana, the taking in of life, of the god, the participation with the divine—even the words animal and spirit grow from the word breath.

"Let me breathe of it," says our Eskimo poem-maker, and then begins: "I have put my poem in order on the threshold of my tongue."

"What poetry expresses," wrote Cassirer, "is neither the mythic word-picture of gods and daemons, nor the logical truth of abstract determinations and relations. The world of poetry stands apart from both, as a world of illusion and fantasy—but it is just in this mode of illusion that the realm of pure feeling can find utterance, and can therewith attain its full and concrete actualization."[3]

A long line of rationale stretches the brain from some cosmic drama and numinous response of primeval nature to the peculiar deadlocks of our printed world. Poetry is a purifying of the semantic contamination of speech. Poetry can bring the mind and its creation full circle, back to unity.

The semantic reality is a projection of abstract verbal concepts. The mind's longing for unity subjects the fragments of its verbal world to logical sequencing, giving a semantic unity of sorts. Existing in imagination, the unity so created has few points of correspondence with our actual ambient of living movements. Through selective inattention we try to shape the ambient in keeping with our ideation, fostering illusions of prediction and control.

In the mirror-to-mirror function of our cocreative mind, our semantic universe tends to become the case—though it collapses into chaos at every hand.

We have created a strange, triple abstraction thrice removed from reality: our use of words divides us from that which we name; we construct a sequence of verbal concepts to weld the fragments into a semblance of semantic unity; and then we concretize, through writing down for visual mirroring, our abstract construct—giving it objective and tangible reality.

The notion of the "linear" as opposed to the cyclic may have arisen from writing. It was surely concretized through printing.[4] The Eskimo can recognize upside down as easily as right-side up, backwards as easily as forwards. We cannot cognize in so free a fashion. Our cognition system orients according to our linear style of print. We left-to-right, timeline our data. We begin this conditioning of our cognition at that period of biological development when operational thinking unfolds. We school the mind into a one-way channel.

Regardless of source, the linear directs our attention away from the present into a split between past and future. "History," as a concretized linear abstraction has a profound effect on each of us. This synthetic drama moves out of an imaginary reconstruction into a fantasized prefiguration. Our life is never seen as a sufficient unit to itself, but of value only in our relation to our invention, history. Our life has authenticity only as we stand in the reflective judgment of things-before and things-to-follow. The present is a hypothesis of value only as it reflects backwards and forwards.

Nothing so beautifully fits the needs of culture as does this "history," and its bastard offspring, progress and evolution. Nothing so moves a man outside his center and into the semantic cauldron.

To the archaic man one's name was one's essence. The ancient Hebrew considered God's name secret. The verbal symbol stood for the real. Nothing has changed. In a semantic world where the word-label denotes the real, the name stands proxy for. In a literate world of imperishable print, one's printed name stands proxy for one's being.

The notion of history cancels out the reality of the eternal present, and gives rise to "immortality," the semantic proxy. Through print, one's *name label* achieves a kind of "immortality." After the invention of music printing, there was no more anonymous music making. Today, self-conscious that his name might "live immortal," the composer writes with one eye on a history of the past, the other on a hoped for history of the future. No eye is left for the now of his audience.

The poet's passion is for print. No longer does it suffice to have the song leap to the tongue for the moment's breathing. The song leaps up and is seized as justification for one's life within the eye of that great jury out-there of history. Art becomes an ace-up-the-sleeve. The leader's attention divides the moment's decision between historical precedence and the image of self to be carried into a name-printed history yet to be written.

(And for the mass of supportive consensus-fillers, a plot of eternal care may have one's *name* emblazoned in everlasting marble, granite, or even bronze–lest we forget or be forgotten–for a small monthly charge.)

In lieu of a present moment in which to be, culture offers a thick treacly substitute of sentiment, memory, and death. Each figure of this unholy trinity spawns the other and blocks us from life.

Don Juan "erases" memory as a block between sense and percept. Jesus urges one to put the shoulder to the plow and not look back. Don Juan shrugs off the shroud of sentiment. Sentiment hangs a past about us as "precious" and to be reversed. Nothing seems sacred to don Juan except life. Jesus says let the dead bury the dead; denies his mother, and speaks of a man's worst enemies as those of his household. Don Juan accepts his death—wrestles with him, joys in the struggle. Jesus urges one to pick up the cross.

These paradigms deride our cloying delusions. Both give up those cultural life-preservers that sink us in a semantic sea. And both move freely into an interaction with a reality "closed to our senses five."

11. Double-Mindedness

And Single Vision

In *Crack,* I postulated two mental modes that I called "autistic thinking," and "reality-adjusted" thinking. I looked for a way these could be expressed physically within the brain system. The German neurological school had postulated that "autistic" thought generated in the old brain system. This implied that reality-adjusted thinking took place in the newer cortex.

Not long after publishing *Crack* I was introduced to the "split-brain" research of Sperry of Cal Tech, and found a fascinating model for the two modes of thinking. I extrapolated heavily on the findings and built up quite a psychological cosmology, only to abandon my head trip later, and consign a new manuscript to the fire.

The split-brain model is esthetically appealing, probably roughly correct, but filled with problems. Briefly, our new brain, or neocortex, is divided into two hemispheres connected by a thick web of nerves called the *corpus callosum.* The purpose of the *corpus callosum* was long unknown, and the reason for two hemispheres only vaguely surmised. The function of each hemisphere has been opened to considerable analysis through what has become known as "split-brain research." Following experiments with animals, the *corpus callosum* connecting the two hemispheres has been severed surgically in several dozen severe epileptic patients. In addition, Brenda Milner of Canada has succeeded in anaesthetizing one hemisphere at a time for brief intervals, and other techniques are being developed.

The "major" hemisphere has been found to have volitional control over the dominant body movements, such as the right hand. This hemisphere controls speech, reading, and writing, thinks analytically and sequentially, and represents our "reality-adjusted" social thinking.

The "minor" hemisphere has no language capacity but seems to "think" in pictures, symbols, and intuitive hunches. This hemisphere conceives holistically, probably constructs the complete patterns from "major" mode sequential, analytical fragments; gives us our spatial orientation (our identity in physical space), and is possibly the source of artistic talents. Finally, it may be more "autistic" in its operations, and seems to be connected with autonomous bodily functions and "body-knowings" of homeostatic nature.

Qualifications and cautions are surely in order concerning any simple model for human thinking. The older German neurological theories can't be dismissed. There are intricate "thinking" systems operating below the limen of awareness. Thinking is an all-inclusive, organismic process, not just a cerebral activity.

We err in identifying function too closely with specific functional parts. Intellect operates through functional parts but never relates in a one-for-one correspondence with any part. Thinking involves the brain, surely, but it also involves the body, and lies finally beyond any medium *for* thinking.

What needs to be emphasized is the infinite complexity of the mind-brain scheme. One brain researcher exclaimed that "the more we discover the less we know." A prominent Canadian neurosurgeon abandoned brain research for this reason. David F. Salisbury, writing in the *Christian Science Monitor,* struck this note of caution. He quoted Worden of M.I.T., who said science confronts in the brain a system "so vast and awe-inspiring that it makes all else simple to the point of triviality." Brodal of the University of Oslo in Norway said, "The more we know about the units of the brain the more complex seems the pattern of their organization." (A decade ago technician mentalities spoke suredly of replicating and even replacing the brain with computers.)

So far all the research on the brain has verified my hypotheses in *Crack,* yet all models so far emerging have fallen short of the magnitude of mind I outlined, and paradoxes crop up continually. I hope to suggest here some of the nature of the mind-brain scheme involved. To do this I must ignore large areas of controversy, as I had to do in *Crack,* for the sake of brevity, and in order to concentrate on the elements of the puzzle germane.

The first difference in the functions of our hemispheres was discovered back in the eighteenth century, when it was found that the "major" hemisphere, the one running the right side of the body, controls *speech.* The "minor" hemisphere has since been found to be very much speechless.

Hemispheric specialization for speech may be tied

in with acculturation and the split of mind. In the child there seems to be *no* specialization of the language act. Both hemispheres are involved in language development and continue to take part in language use for the first seven or eight years. By the time the child has reached nine or ten years of age, however (*note the date*), one of the hemispheres *takes over* the speech function entirely–usually the left or "major" hemisphere. At this time speech atrophies in the minor lobe. Brain damage to the major hemisphere after that point cannot be speech-compensated by the minor mode.

This may well be the result of cultural conditioning acting on an inherent biological tendency, and emphasizing that tendency out of proportion. It may well be a biological *reaction* on the part of our natural, Primary Program. Let me state this possibility briefly and prematurely, trusting it will clarify later:

In his earlier work, Sperry had shown that there exists a precise "chemical coding system" during brain growth, that allows specific nerve cells to find their way through the tangle of other fibers. For instance, cells involved in vision would "find their way through" to link with their proper nerve fibers in the appropriate spot, even when obstacles were arbitrarily induced to block the normal routes.

Individual living heart cells, isolated on a microscopic slide, pulse at varying tempos. Brought closer together, at a certain point they will begin to pulse in rhythmic unison–functioning as a heart. Somehow they have "communicated" across the intervening spaces and established "identity."

These examples could be multiplied at length. Are we to consider such remarkable symbiotic relations and communications, that can overcome even great odds to *fulfill prescribed roles,* as incidental effects of cells only?

Our biological organism functions as planned, even though obstacles are placed in the path. One brain organ, for instance, might have to *reject* language activity in order to keep intact its prescribed role for which it was designed. When language activity begins to work in ways blocking the original intent, the "minor" mode ceases that activity.

Consider that around nine years of age when the child can construct the "death concept," cultural abstractions begin directly affecting the interactions with reality. This is the period when the "peer-group" effect begins to operate and the acculturation drive fully opens. This is the period when language operations shift to the major hemisphere.

Cultural logic is a semantic affair that fragments subject from object and categorizes the world into discrete and separate parts. Literacy tends to name-label and categorize, and fragment into a time-line sequence. The act of reading breaks meaning, logic, and the reality picture ensuing into discrete segments occurring sequentially. This effect can't be handled by a function designed for gestalt holistic grasp, but *is* suited to the "major" modes analytical breaking down.

Finally, the "minor" mode may be our connection with the flow of life, and our silent "body-knowings." As language becomes counter to this primary perception, the function may shut out language in order to keep intact its symbiotic relations of a nonverbal order.

So the part of the neocortex designed for logical processing and analytical breakdown is given over to cultural conditioning as a survival necessity. Under acculturation, each hemisphere assumes that role most natural to its functions and adjusts to the cultural demands accordingly. The self-system might still employ techniques for balancing the two modalities, and using each in its proper phase according to need, but even this "phasing" breaks down under the extremes of cultural conditioning.

Back to "split-brain" research, no one involved has suggested that a comprehensive knowledge of the minor mode exists, and even our notions of, "major" mode activity might be subject to revision. The shortcomings of sharp, clear-cut, mechanical dichotomies in such a mysterious process are apparent. Robert Ornstein points out that much of our current information has come from patients with severe brain disorders. Our data might not be typical. With reservations, though, the metaphors and analogies afforded prove helpful, and enough evidence converges for certain general assumptions.

The left hemisphere is called the "major" one since it controls the right side of the body, and indirectly most of the volitional system of "purposeful" acitivity. This major mode that runs the right side of the body might "dominate" the system, but it is surely not the most important. It thinks in linear sequency, handles language and logical processing, all of which are vital to acculturation. Not surprisingly, then, this hemisphere seems the seat of our social ego.

Were language only poetic or communicative, were it never used other than to express those thoughts "sung out with the breath when people are moved by great forces . . . when the words we want shoot up of themselves . . ." (it breathing one) language might never link with the analytical processes. Language as poetry communicates wholes, spiritual responses to the flow of life. In that form, language could remain a characteristic of the "minor" mode as well as major. It would be interesting, for instance, to test our nonliterate Eskimo poets for speech domination of hemisphere. For hemispheric speech-separation might be found only in literate, abstract cultures.[1]

Language is used as a tool for cultural logic to create those buffers to the fear created *by* cultural logic. These buffers necessarily block off the "life-flow" system as well, contributing to the specialization of hemispheres. Indications are strong that no cultural logic functions in a fully conceptual manner as a mediant between sense and percept until preadolescense, somewhere after six and before twelve to fourteen. It is not fortuitous that roof-brain chatter and the peer-group effect become active during this stage, shifting the person toward social consensus.

From adolescence, both language and operational thinking orient to verbal logic and the semantic scheme. Cultural-logic fuses language to propositional logic, and creates the semantic reality function.

Each hemisphere of the brain, according to Sperry, develops a distinct personality. The personality of the major mode is, as stated, our social ego, aware self. The right hemisphere apparently develops a personality, too, but being mute, it remains elusive. Split-brain patients report the puzzling feeling of "having someone else in my head with me."

The minor hemisphere seems to be the mode that recognizes faces. Recall that the infant is born with the innate ability to pick out and focus his eyes on a human face. From this known orientation point he could then branch out to other objects, leading to his development of object-constancy and the beginnings of true reality interaction. The one "known" with which we are born thus carries with it the germ of all the rest of the pattern of knowing that will develop.

Consider, however, that the *corpus callosum* is not developed until around age two. Were the *corpus callosum* the only way for hemispheric interchange, then we must consider that object-constancy, symbolization, and all the logical development of the first two years occurred in only the minor hemisphere—which is doubtful indeed. Perhaps the hemispheres exchanged functional products through older brain formations before development of the connecting *corpus callosum*. Or face recognition and symbolic processing may have been, like language, an equal ability of both hemispheres.

So specialization of the hemispheres might be a development of acculturation, not an endowment from the beginning. No specialization is known to exist in the brains of animals, and they seem to possess a symbiotic relation with the Flow. So do children, until hemispheric specialization. Yet hemispheric specialization is obviously biological and necessary for development of operational thinking. Culture fosters this specialization even as it channels it. Language, however, might not necessarily have to be so divided.

In split-brain patients, the major hemisphere's "personality" (our ordinary social self) refuses to admit the presence or actions of the minor hemisphere from which it is severed. Yet the ego doing the talking will make apologies for, or rationalize, the actions made by the left hand (over which it then has no control). In the same way, the minor mode registers actual irritation at the lack of holistic grasp the major mode displays. The left hand of such patients will reach out to correct the right hand's fumbling efforts in tasks requiring a grasp of the whole. Physical conflict between the two hands will actually take place.

Ornstein points out that children from poor black neighborhoods learn to use their right hemispheres more than their left. They outscore white children on tests of pattern recognition from incomplete figures, even as they do poorly in verbal tasks. Carpenter notes the same capacity among the Eskimo, who grasp pattern intuitively.

The Eskimo are uncanny mechanics–a simple glance at the most sophisticated machine and they simply understand its workings and can quickly repair a malfunction. (We hear reports of "idiot-savants," who can do fantastic mathematical computations but can not read or write.) Overemphasis of verbal thinking tends to diminish one's abilities for free movement of body and pattern grasp.

Nevertheless, all our neat dichotomizing falls into difficulties. Einstein reports that he rarely thought in words at all for his original ideas. "A thought comes, and I may try to express it in words afterwards." His ideas first appeared in what he called "physical entities," images and symbols he could reproduce and combine. He spoke of these elements as being "visual," and even of *muscular type*. Don Juan would speak of body-knowing, and I would refer to Tart's experiment given in the first chapter, where the subject's "body" knew, but his "awareness" didn't. I would also remind *Crack* readers of my lengthy examples and illustrations of the arrival of the Eureka! answer found in all great scientific discoveries. These answers always arrived in symbolic form, which then had to be translated.

Einstein said that conventional words or other signs had to be sought for laboriously only in a secondary stage, when the mentioned associative play was sufficiently established and could be reproduced at will.

Lest it be presumed that Einstein was thus a "right-hemisphere" thinker, recall that he was a mathematician, surely thought analytically, and is labeled a "scientist." He spoke of his original ideas coming to him, *arriving*. Analytical work preceded and proceeded from these Eureka! experiences; which could be considered from the "minor" mode.[2]

The point is that creative, original thinking comes from a play of the modalities of the mind-brain, not from one or the other operating in exclusion. William Blake claimed that only through discipline, analytical and fragmenting as it may be, could the truly original ideas break through and be translated into reality.

Mozart surely conceived of his great works in Gestalt wholes, and wrote them out intact without corrections being needed. He could, further, once having conceived a piece and worked it out in his head, play it thereafter without writing it down at all, a practice he often followed with his piano concerti.

We tend to ignore, however, the enormous discipline of Mozart's mind. We tend to overlook his own lament that he was taken to be a kind of machine, that no one realized how intensely hard he had to work at composing. Both "areas" of his brain were surely involved. The "concept" of a piece arrived as a total gestalt, but he had to work out the "note translation" in his head. Once his "headwork" was done, he could simply write out the notes without hesitation.

Mozart would even have his wife read to him

as he wrote out a score, to occupy his mind that he might more freely copy out that which he had already composed in his head. Now I suppose we can relate all this to major-minor hemispheres, but the going gets sticky. Music, according to split-brain research, is a minor hemisphere activity. (Ornstein proposes EEG biofeedback training of the minor hemisphere as a means of promoting creativity.) Mozart's right hand had to do the transcribing of notes onto paper, so a "crossover" of modes is indicated. His major mode also would have done the analytical part of note translation, perhaps. Yet he gets his wife to read to him—words, a major-mode activity, in order that his right hand, under that major mode, might more freely copy out what his left-handed thinking originated.

Ornstein has a simple test in which one balances a pencil while talking. The balance is less difficult with the left hand, since the right hand is doing the talking and can't divide its attention well. So, with Mozart—well, he was copying notes from his minor-mode with his major-mode hand, but to do this freely he occupied that major-mode with storytelling to keep it out of the way—except for copying those notes of course, from his minor-hemisphere, except he was listening to a story with his right-hand mind, or was that mind listening to his left-handed music making—(at which point a *petit-mal* epileptic seizure splits my brain).

Whether this is apropos or not, consider that both Mozart and Einstein were poorly adjusted to "reality." Einstein was quite "fey" and inept at what we consider common-sense practicalities; and had Mozart been better acculturated he would no doubt have survived the irrationalities of his culture longer, and we would have had more great music. Neither Einstein nor Mozart were school products. Mozart had no formal schooling at all, and yet picked up different languages, and as his letters alone indicate, was sophisticated and erudite for his time. (Irrationality is the best protection in an irrational world. One needs to learn to survive–discipline must encompass the irrational to be free for the rationality of creation.)

Mozart and Einstein display certain avenues of uncluttered response between the modes of mind. Intensive education almost surely thwarts this flow. Natural thought is a balance of the two modes of mind. The idea that art and music emerge from the minor hemisphere is misleading. The idea that biofeedback could train one to use the right hemisphere and so induce creativity remains to be seen. A short two years or so ago the same enthusiasm was registered over producing Alpha states through biofeedback and attaining a Zen-master state in a few short weeks.

Sir John Eccles considers major-mode thinking to be the "supreme human achievement." He calls language that which is "truly human." Eccles considers language thinking the only kind of thinking. He makes a clear distinction between "consciousness of sounds and smells," and *thinking*. He splits not only the body and mind, but intellect itself, in typical academic fashion.

Einstein's thought contradicts Eccles, as does any artists. (William Blake claimed that no one could be a [Blake] Christian, that is, a vehicle for the "divine imagination," unless he were a poet, a painter, architect or musician. He excluded Newton, but he might have accepted an Einstein.)

Verbal thinking assumes a dominance with which it is incompetent to deal. The irrational aspects of our culture result from this very error. Verbal thinking in the acculturated mind can only interact with the semantic reality of culture. Were this act not taken to be naturally dominant, and given divine sanction by the social scheme, it could be a creative modality. As it is, verbal thinking is the "fall" of man, and the split of mind.

Verbal thinking is only one aspect of thinking, and thinking is only one aspect of consciousness. Verbal thinking can mask the wider plays of consciousness. Carrington once stated that individual consciousness was "contained within a field of consciousness." Edgar Mitchell, the former astronaut, spoke of the universe as *being* consciousness. Don Juan, Jesus, the Zen Master take this as axiomatic. You can't say the flower or plant *has* consciousness–it *is* consciousness. Consciousness is not an "essence" added to or emanating from. Consciousness is an act, a process of being. In her remarkable study, *Mind, an Essay on Human Thinking,* Susanne Langer demonstrates that every life process is an act of thinking, that thinking always expresses as a process of being.

Our dominant verbal mode of thinking tunes the body senses toward social-semantic actions. This linguistic mode further generates "roof-brain chatter" as one of its homeostatic stabilizers of the semantic reality. Those sensory levels of a nonsemantic nature are drowned out and ignored.

The social-semantic process not only screens out data from a "real world" in order to keep the semantic structure intact, but it screens out senses generated internally which are not related to its own control. Just as with the split-brain patient whose hands literally struggled with each other over dominance, the social ego retains its "hierarchy of mind."

(The frustrations of "psychic" investigators trying to "prove" their validity to conservative or scientifically oriented people is analogous.)

The nonverbal modes of mind are probably unfathomable. Memory, for instance, was long considered, and I suppose still is, to be an electro-chemical kind of molecular-cellular activity. Wilder Penfield found that stimulation of certain areas of the temporal lobe triggered memories of music in some patients, often whole phrases. Audition seems connected with the temporal lobe as sight is connected with the occipital lobe. But such "memories" are unrelated fragments. As yet, no known place or even way is evident by which the mind perceives whole images or events, and yet we perceive in unbroken wholes.

That the body itself has a memory system is not generally acknowledged (and it will surely work out differently from the rough pattern I suggested previously). That memory is *not limited* to molecular-cellular activity is almost certainly the case, though molecules and cells are obviously involved. All the senses are drawn on to shape any percept. Sight, for instance, is known to be highly "synthetic," utilizing all the senses. And memory, regardless of its imperfections and errors, is an end product of a thinking act. We do not "turn our minds loose on a memory," but act mentally in such a fashion.

In memory the intellect connects its datum into a unit according to pattern as in all acts of thinking. Arcing the gaps of past experience can be quite faulty. Were memories "stored as units," such errors would be less likely to happen. Object-constancy and homeostatic "stable-sameness" backgrounds are a kind of "memory" on which general cognition calls at every instant. Even our ordinary vision can at times be faulty in the same way a memory can.

For instance, I went into my bank carrying the key case for my car. It was a large, light blue, leather affair, about the size of a wallet. I put the case on the counter as I wrote a check. Turning to go I could not find the case. No one else had been standing there. There was, on the counter, a very small triangular black key case, the kind that snaps tightly over two keys at the most. Puzzled, I looked around for who might have taken my keys and left theirs. The cashier asked what was wrong, and I explained that my car keys were missing. "But there is your key case," she said, pointing to the foreign, little, black, triangular-shaped counterfeit. "No, ma'am" I said, pushing the strange case away, "my case is large, light blue, etc. etc." "But that *is* a blue case, and you put it there," the poor girl insisted, looking genuinely concerned. Again I turned to the foreign object and instantly reperceived it as, indeed, a large, blue leather case. Confused, I picked it up and left.

Later that day I suddenly remembered that little case. In my early student days I had chauffeured for three years for a very old and dear little lady, and those were the keys to her car. I knew them as well as my hand. I knew then that cognition was subject to variables. Such an error of pattern-recognition-name-labeling or whatever may have been connected with my distracted state, following a severe personal loss. But I knew after that that men have been hung on less substantial memory "evidence."

The kinds of memory created by Penfield's electrical stimulation of the brain are intriguing fragments. This gives no proof, however, that memory is exclusively cerebral. Ida Rolfe reactivated a complete sensory replay of an entire event in John Lilly's life by manipulating the scar-tissue on his foot. Are we then to presume that memory really resides in our feet?

Neither the mind-brain memory system nor its sensory system is limited to one's personal background. Precognition, for instance, is a fairly common phenomenon. Louisa Rhine has file cabinets full of such performances, and surely most of us could contribute our fair share. Precognition must be considered the other side of the coin from memory. They are both aspects of the same phenomena. Whether involved in the postcognition of memory, or the "extrasensory" perception of "precognition," the mind participates in a sweeping continuum of event.

Memory is seriously impaired when the *corpus callosum* is cut. The subdominant hemisphere may be vital not just for recalling one's "personal history" but as the link with the continuum of experience called the Flow. The entire homeostatic network is involved in memory, but probably of a most general sort. When we consciously act as a remembering intellect, we may put together a most imperfect kind of record.

Under Kirlian photography a dying leaf slowly loses its "aura" effect. Don Juan "saw" his dying son's life exploding out into the world, as fragments of shooting light. Where go the "lights?" Perhaps the Flow is a memory of sorts.

12. I-not-I

Some half dozen of us met regularly over an extended period, experimenting along the "mind-games" line. This was before Masters-Houston's book, *Mind Games,* was available, but we did have Charles Tart's *Altered States of Consciousness.* We developed a considerable rapport and emotional bond. Connecting ideas from various sources, we decided that if we could "park" the body, and yet keep the mind alert, we could by-pass our world-view grid and experience nonordinary reality.

We used trance induction procedures developed at Stanford, as well as the "Stanford Scale" to indicate trance depth. We found, as I had pointed out in *Crack,* that none of us initiated action in trance. We could respond verbally to a question, for instance, but never asked one. Without suggestions or questions from someone we simply stayed in our body-parked limbo. So one of us stayed in the ordinary state and acted as guide for our adventures.

At a certain depth of trance we found that we could, were the suggestion given, spontaneously create and entertain vivid dreams that were like hypnagogic states. When one member was asked to create such a dream, others tended to "pick up" on the dream and enter into it as participants—which fact would be perceived by the initiator.

Tart produced similar results with two graduate students, a male and female. Their nonordinary experiences became so compellingly real that the young man involved withdrew since his shared nonordinary states seemed as tangible as his ordinary world. As Carlos would say, he could no longer guarantee himself consensus on what was real.

In our experiments, an adventure into "telepathy" indicated the relating of the two modes of mind. I was acting as guide and had brought some large geometric figures drawn with ruler and compass. These were in a manila folder and had been seen by no one else.

When all trance conditions had been met, I brought out the drawings, one at a time, looked at them briefly, and asked the group to report if they "saw" anything. Each immediately responded yes, and, as was evident, each perceived the figure. (They were, of course, all sprawled about, body-parked, eyes closed.)

In translating what they saw into communicable form, however, certain subtle and significant changes were manifested—changes that gave clear indication of the relating of the modes of mind.

One of the figures, for instance, was a circle with a square cross in it, made thus:

Each "sensed" the figure, but in "perceiving" the figure, or in translating it into the common domain, their perceptions of that figure took intriguing variations.

My taciturn, practical friend from New England "saw" a wagon wheel in which the spokes didn't come together as they should. Our esthetic musician-artist saw a flower blossom from the stem side, the four large sepals fringed about with a circle of petals. His wife saw a circle with a cross *under* it, the universal symbol of the female, fittingly enough.

When I looked at the figure of a triangle with a circle inside it, the group produced: the trylon and perisphere from the old New York World's Fair; the great pyramid with a globe of the earth on top; the capitol letter *A* with a small *o* inside; and so on.

The telepathic dream research of Drs. Ullman and Krippner was suggested through an experience of Dr. Ullman's. A woman patient had been to see the doctor for her regular weekly session at a rather late hour. On parting, Dr. Ullman had gone to a lecture demonstration concerning the inducing of alcoholism in *cats*. Dr. Ullman was intrigued by a film in which alcoholic cats turned down various foods in favor of milk heavily laced with alcohol.

The following week his lady patient reported a strange dream which she had on retiring the very evening of the lecture and film. She had dreamed of being in her kitchen with her husband, seated at the table. Before them was a strange mixture of an alcoholic nature. This was disturbing since the husband's fondness for drink was one of the domestic tensions. Then the scene slightly shifted in dream-sequence style, and in place of the strange alcoholic drink, there on the table was a basket with kittens in it.

The coincidence led Dr. Ullman into his now famous research on telepathic influence of dreams. Suffice here to note that a patient's "transference" to analyst is well known; "unconscious exchange" is generally marked in such relations, and an emotional link is usual.

The specific content of the film was not "transferred" to the patient's dream. She drew on only those components that matched corresponding material from her own unique frame of reference. She translated from sensory input into cognitive perception according to her current set of attention. This proved to be the case in all subsequent experiments of this nature. Even in nonordinary sense-perception, one does not cognize directly, but re-cognizes according to established patterns.

So it was in our little group. The sensory input was turned into perception, as all sensory input must be—through translation by the cognitive system, which is unique to each of us.

"Telepathy" is a misnomer. Nothing is "sent." There is no broadcasting through the ether of brain waves to be picked up by "mental radios." There is no mysterious X Force or psi-plasma awaiting our discovery and control. Our models from technology are misleading.

In our group experiments, we partially suspended the ordinary semantic screening of mind. (Only partially, since communication was still possible, though perfunctory and limited.) We had parked the body by stilling muscle tonus and suspending the postures, stances, and gestures of social identity. Thus we suspended our ordinary reality checks, identifications, and not incidentally, roof-brain chatter. Simultaneously, we had, by agreement, alerted our senses to the possibility of just such an exchange as did occur. We had selected the elements desired and suspended the conflicting possibilities. We had, in effect, curbed semantic dominance to some extent, and had set up the conditions for the kind of mediating that could take place between sense and percept.

That portion of my ordinary sensing that pertained to the experiment was, by agreement, a group stimulus. My "roof-brain" activity had nothing to do with the performance other than as my "intent." To use split-brain terminology, the "minor" mode apparently doesn't transfer fragmented bits and pieces, but gestalt wholes, symbols, pictures, or events. Just as the shared dream tended to be picked up and entered into by other members, so had this specific aspect of my cognition.

My sensory activity pertaining to the group was automatically their sense data. Their perceiving of that sensory intake was unique to each, however, since, again, a percept is an end product of thinking. Even though "parked," their ordinary processes were needed for the final portion of the cognitive act, and their unique self-systems gave unique results.

Ordinary semantic-ego thinking is restricted to its own modality and constructs. The relation with the universal "minor" mode is rather a street up which ego-aware me can't go. All I can do is set up the conditions by which traffic may or very well may not move back in my direction. For, inadvertently, and unbeknownst, my setting up of the conditions for my survival in my social world has blocked that traffic in the first place.

The "minor" mode may respond and may not. This minor mode can obviously "move both ways." This area of mind is connected with "body-knowing." It is also the seat of emotions and "senses" the attitudes and sets of "major" mode thinking. Analogous to this was Carlos's "conversations" with the coyote. One can translate such exchanges into paraphrased words, but actually no language is involved.

My intellect can only set up conditions. The other modality picks, screens, or responds as needed, desired, or able. I don't know which. The language barrier seems evident, but can evidently be overcome as needed. Nonambiguity, or "unbending intent" can bridge the gap at times. The relation is a mystery.

Still (the question persists), granted an "extrasensory" perception took place, how did the group "sense" the datum in the first place?

As guide, I initiated the response by looking at the drawing. I furnished the group with a stimulus in the same way that ordinary symbolic formation gives a stimulus substitution in the absence of the actual object. The mental act of perception was then completed by their regular processes much as in ordinary symbolic thinking. The difference was that the stimulus came from my looking, rather than having been created in their own symbolic system.

Again, though, how did they pick up the stimulus itself, substituted or not?

Their images formed as symbolic imagery forms in the absence of direct stimuli. The image formed in their nonverbal, "minor" mode of mind, as all such imagery and recognition of such imagery does. For, as my semantic, social-ego mode of thinking is unique to me, my nonverbal "minor" mode is nonpersonal and a commonly shared process. The one in my head is in some way the same one functioning in your head. By selective attention, pertinent elements in my cognitive process were automatically elements in my friend's process.

It is established that telepathic phenomena generally are perceived in symbol, patterns, pictures. Even "messages" that translate into words are generally grasped as a whole entity needing translation. "Extrasensory perception" is thus, like telepathy, a misnomer. An extrasensory perception is no more "extra" than any symbolic formation. It simply generates at a further step removed from ego awareness.

"Paranormal" phenomena indicates for us that our nonverbal modes of mind, wherever they might "reside," have not been split from our natural state of communion, and have not been metaprogrammed by culture. The Primary Process, and our Primary Program, thus remain intact in this modality.

"Diversity in unity" is a clue. For instance, why, if one opens to a continuum of thinking in trance, did our group pick up just the geometric drawings? Why did Tart's subject pick up only those body-knowing events it did and not, say, a severe trauma occurring elsewhere? Why did strange events happen to Carlos in the desert only when accompanied by don Juan (at least at first)? Why did Jesus propose that two or three could gather together and "agreeing" on what they asked, receive accordingly?

Aldous Huxley spoke of "mind at large," Jung of a "collective unconscious," James of "other consciousnesses all about us." A model of a vast cosmic "storehouse" of information or data begins to emerge. Our brains are then seen as "valves" filtering from this what we need for survival. This can be very misleading. As a flexible model such ideas are workable, but as theories they are problematic.

Tart's subject picked up the "sender's" body reactions because that is what the experiment was designed for. My group picked up from me according to the structuring provided. Carlos picks up from the desert differently when with don Juan since he is living in don Juan's "unconscious" much as a child with a parent. Don Juan is the dominant modality. Forks bend in Yuri Geller's presence or influence (though differing from don Juan, he doesn't know why).

Spiritualist "call up spirits." I have no doubt Arthur Ford "called up" James Pike's dead son. That's what the experiment was for. They received "evidential material" that couldn't have been rigged. That is what they were after. The "information" was "there," but where is "there"? *There* is in the act itself, in that particular kind of transaction with reality, that kind of intellectual interaction with possibility. Their very acts, their interactions, may have "produced" the "son" material, much as a Tibetan produces a tulpa figure, or very much as don Juan produces the spirit of the water hole. When that kind of transaction is over, that kind of event might be over. An ordinary traveler passing that water hole perceives no spirits, since he is not interacting with reality in that way.

We set up an experiment or a situation and we put into motion a set of expectancies. By scientific procedure, will, intent, or "claim," we transact accordingly. We "arc the gaps" of data according to the needs of that pattern. But, as with the quantum leap and the orbit assumed for its traversal, our act of arcing the gap between the data may be the activating of the data in that manner as well. The arc across the gap and the data resulting may be "quantumlike" events.

I can set up conditions that may or may not induce a response from this silent half of my self, but I can't enter into this area of mind and engineer the results. This silent mode apparently "picks up" from my intellect and deposits there ad lib. It may deposit "extrasensory" kinds of possibility for perception. Some of its "pick-ups" from me, such as my passionate commitment questions, may occasionally return as those mighty "Eureka!" wholes, beyond the creative ability of my analytical processes. Either type of these interactions of mind must await those odd break-points in *my* noisy major-mode activity.

The silent, minor mode might offer many a deposit ordinarily turned down by our roof-brained ego. The right hand of a patient whose brain had been split by surgery tore down the holistic result given by his left hand in an experiment. The right hand of the patient physically fought off the efforts of the left hand to correct the fragmented failures of the right. The minor mode might offer an enormous variety of sense-data for full perceiving which the grid effect of the acculturated mind screens out. The tenaciousness of the fear-ridden ego-self's dominance is not to be taken lightly.

Extrasensory perception and paranormal phenomena in no way indicate the nature of our Primary Programs. The "psychic" who has access to certain kinds of interactions in no way suggests a person who is no longer culturally dominated and under his Primary Program. Paranormal phenomena is only roughly indicative of primary perception or primary processing.

My intellect can't enter this other mode of mind, but the other mode is always a functional part of my intellect. The discoveries of split-brain research offer a neat model for creative thinking as I outlined in *Crack*: the asking of the question and commitment to the answer; the search for materials; the unconscious synthesis; the logical exhaustion and moment off guard, and the arrival of the Eureka! answer "out of the blue." The answer "arcs the gap" and arrives in consciousness. This very well may be a "crossing of the corpus callosum." At any rate such imagery is effective analogically.

Split-brain patients have extreme difficulty with new learning and memory. Consider, however, that over a period of time, certain compensations begin to function. Learning apparently gets re-routed after a fashion. Faced with a problem needing bilateral cooperation between hemispheres, split-brain patients can, with patience and persistence, sometimes learn to solve such a problem. Their results might be slow and arduous, but partial compensations are indicated.

Recall that Sperry's earlier work revealed how brain cells would reroute themselves and overcome arbitrarily induced obstacles that blocked their ordinary linkage with their proper system. Both hemispheres of the neocortex are connected with the older brain organs, of course. And thinking tends to be an all-inclusive process. Our computer analogies do not wear well in the long run. Modes of function are never exactly synonymous with functional parts, and life proves remarkably adaptive and versatile.

What I have tried to suggest in these few examples is that the mode of mind functioning as "autistic" or "primary processing," is far more than the simple mechanics offering themselves to "major-mode" probes.

No combination of "minor hemisphere," "old-brain," and "body-knowing" thinking processes can account for the scope of creative thinking. When Einstein's answers arrived, they may have "crossed the corpus callosum," but they encompassed universal principles lying far outside his personal ken. Yet, as Blake said, a cup can't conceive beyond its own capaciousness, and in the resulting paradox lies a key for us. Our "shadow-side" of brain-mind is both personal and more than personal. At some point my thinking contains more than myself.

"Psychics" and clairvoyants who can open to some aspects of "continuum thinking" are often flooded with impressions that flow swiftly through them. Their problem is to "seize" on a particular impression and hold to it. That chosen impression then acts as an orientation for related material. They have then created a set of expectancy, a pattern by which to interact with data.

Our two modes of mind are designed for these different functions. Ordinarily we orient to that which is pertinent to our individual experience and cultural set. Robert Jeffries proposed that spontaneous telepathy generally occurs from close emotional bonds. This is what makes cold, analytical laboratory experimenting difficult.

Examples abound: A Navy flyer's pet dog suddenly awoke at 3:00 A.M., howling terribly. He had never before done such a thing, and the flyer's wife could not calm him or shut him up. Later that morning she was informed of the 3:00 A.M. crash and death of her husband.

Within our "minor mode" abides the universal. The affinity of children and animals, a primary perception in plants, and all the "paranormal" phenomena occur since there is only one Primary Process. The one in my head is the one in your's and in the dog's head as well, in its canine expression. We draw on it and contribute to it in myriads of ways outside ordinary awareness.

Primary perception is a different matter from Primary Processing by one point. A primary sense-datum must be translated through the world-view grid of the semantic system to be a percept. (This presumes a sensing of that datum by the overloaded ego-system in the first place.) And our semantic function translates the input according to conditioning and individual intent. No two experiences of the Primary Process could ever be identical. The Primary Process is the field from which all our experience arises, but my Primary Program is mine alone and will never be repeated again. Diversity within unity is the cosmic theme, as found in physics and all art.

Developing an ego self-system is the only way of creating the diverse experience from the field of possibility. To accomplish this doesn't have to result in the acculturated semantic ego. Rather, such a cultural product defeats the scheme of nature. The cultural split is the result of an inherent risk in an act of separation *necessary* for the whole maneuver. There is nothing to prevent the cocreative effect so brought about from creating a semantic mediant as it does. We are dealing with creative principles, not divine personalities and edicts.

We err in thinking "ego" an error of the system. My ego is *me,* this diverse and unique creative act arising from the ground of consciousness underlying all things. My ego self-system may be locked into a semantic construction, and the original biological division of labor in the mind-brain scheme may have become a psychosomatic split—but all this is an illusory error, a creation of imagination, no matter how well entrenched. The self-system can shift dominance from culture to Primary Processing by intent. My ego *can* organize around a single focus of intent and override cultural dominance.

Exactly how the two hemispheric brain functions enter into Primary Process and cultural functioning can't be drawn too clearly. Provided we keep our categories flexible and open, such a model can make our analysis easier. Then we can say that the "major" hemisphere is my ego-aware social self. My "minor" hemisphere is also me, mine, here in my head, and yet, at some crucial point no longer me, not my possession and not mine to do with in any of my conditioned ways. Only as we can be ultimately responsible can our interactions open to wide fields as with Jesus or don Juan. The principles by which the cosmos moves are not amenable to change by the whims of our social self.

Never at any point in either ordinary or nonordinary reality experience can you ignore the translating effect on what might be "coming in" from outthere to what is finally perceived "in-here." Nor can the effect be measured by any ordinary method. Whatever we finally perceive at any time is a conglomerate of individual and commonly held possibilities. Don Juan always knew when Carlos was caught up in a "nonordinary" event, but he never pretended for a moment to know the specifics of that event as it transpired.

Our "minor" mode appears more "netti-netti" than anything else. It is not-this, not-that. It is nonsemantic, nonlogical, nonabstracting, nonindividual, nondivisive, non-subject-object, non-cause-effect, non-space-time. Further, if our ordinary thinking represents "reality thinking" and the harsh necessities of survival, this nonordinary thinking represents creativity and play.

Creativity is always expressing in-spite-of. We recognize products of creativity and desire to reproduce them with social-semantic means and for cultural ends. That is, we try to seize this flow capacity as a technique for prediction and control *of* that flow. Man's history has been this folly. We want to possess this nonordinary possibility with our ordinary mind. Possession is a product of cultural conditioning. It is based on fear of loss, which is an expression of the death concept. The attempt to possess is the desire to predict and control that which is possessed, and it is this act that alienates. Rather than shifting the self-system's dominance, we try to force or trick the Primary Process into compliance with our culturally induced grid. Bruner listed the fourth and final step of the creative process as the willingness to be dominated by and serve that which we are involved with. True science does this and cooperates with principles. Technology doesn't necessarily, and can create havoc.

In the flow all is relation and unity. Communion is our natural state. Everything possesses everything else. Don Juan was serious when he gave Carlos the mountain. It was don Juan's to give as much as anyone's. Possession is a semantic illusion overlaid on a buffer device. (On the other hand, there is no moral-ethical virtue in "nonpossession." Denial, in this sense, is a meaningless gesture, as don Juan and Jesus make clear.)

Let me wind this section up with an analogy of the body as a microcosm for that macrocosm in which we live, a way in which diversity in unity operates.

Millions of cells group together mysteriously into perfectly functioning units with widely differing shapes and purposes–such as liver, pancreas, thyroid, heart, gut, and so on. In a natural state the system is complete and designed to function perfectly. The system operates for the maximum good of each of its parts, and each part functions for the maximum good of each of its subparts. Each cell operates for the maximum good of its part and so on back up to the total. Every need is met within the system. The system seems designed only to produce and fill its own needs. Its needs can be infinite, and the system's optimum is abundance and fullness.

The system is impartial in its functioning. All is symbiotic, no part can exist outside the whole, as the whole is nonexistent except as the sum of its parts. A perfect functioning requires a perfect balance and relating of the parts. All parts "give themselves" to the whole in order that their maximum needs might be met.

Should some heart cells decide to be individualistic and operate independently, outside the flow, they could wreck the system. Occasionally it happens, indeed, that a block of cells rebel against the dominance of the flow. A cancer results. This cancer can be called a "cultural effect" since it cultivates only more of itself and at the expense of the whole. Everything loses under this effect.

The system has no preferences, for everything is equally needed, and "right." Yet some body cells are qualitatively different from others. For instance, many cell types are expendable, such as those of the skin and blood. They are continually being replaced. The liver can regenerate portions of itself.

Other cells are strangely irreplaceable, such as those

of the heart, lungs, and brain. And the total system gives a priority rating to these nonreplaceable cells. Oxygen, for instance, will be diverted from other units and kept going to the brain-group as long as possible.

The system is impartial toward its parts, yet perfect functioning depends upon a dominance among those parts. The roles to be played by each are qualitatively different. Yet, paradoxically, only in the equality of all is the system whole.

Certain brain groups, in their unit functioning, might be considered the "thinkers" for the system. And yet this has to be highly qualified. The brain group that "thinks" in this way, or sees itself in this role, is not involved in this way.

The governing of the physical system's autonomous processes is carried on at the base of the brain, in the "old brain." Roof-brain thinking is fortunately free of such an infinitely contingent process. "Thinking" along-brain lines isn't designed for and doesn't enter into the running of any but some volitional aspects of the system.

In fact, thinking in this roof-brain way doesn't enter into any of the mysterious communication that creates the perfect whole from the myriad of diverse parts. "It" breathes the body in this respect. "It" is the whole greater than the sum of its parts, a creative principle expressing as "thinking organism."

Consider, though, that "it" breathing the system does give this neocortical portion a high priority in the system. The priority given is not so high as that given to the autonomic system operating out of the older brain processes, however.

When Carlos realizes that he and the beetle are equals in that they both must die, the coyote can at that point communicate with Carlos. And yet it is immediately apparent that the system gives Carlos superiority in the long run, dominance over beetle and coyote. For what? Surely not to exterminate beetle and coyote as we are wont to do.

So man is, perhaps, the "brain" in the larger body of man, or at least in this earth-body portion of the life-flow system. But note that man is only half that brain, so to speak, only one hemisphere of a dual system. He has volitional control over the volitional aspects of the system, but no real control over the system.

Acculturation is a splitting of the corpus callosum. Man, the half-brain, forgets the "flow" of the system. He forgets that the blood comes from the heart. Or he denies the existence of the system. Being nonverbal, the system is not amenable to semantic mediation and metaphoric mutation, and is thus beyond prediction and control. Or, through analysis, man discovers the operations of the "old brain" and decides those autonomous procedures should be governed by the same "editorial hierarchy" running the semantic show. Or, becoming aware of the heart, man becomes aware that it might fail—so he rigs up a heart machine.

And so we introduce the final madness of the social-ego intellect's attempt to take over all processes. We introduce biofeedback, the attempt to subject every conceivable particle of being to ego-intellectual dominance. (My God! Where is blood cell #10,896,947 *now?*) We have tried to do this with nature-out there, thoroughly fouling it up, and now we try to import the madness within.

Our system of volitional choice may be an outgrowth of the flight-fight response that chooses between two alternatives. This simple either-or logic presumes to be able to attend to and regulate an infinitely contingent process. The simple juggler who has managed to keep two plates in the air suddenly takes on millions of them. Madness.

No matter how irrational and schizoid the cultural mind, it enters as a cocreative force in the reality with which it must then live. The semantic system set up in place of the flow stays in continual chaos since there are an infinite number of variables, impossible for a limited logic to grasp and order into sequence. The cocreative split-mind then tries to repair the damage of its own split functioning. But a split function can do no more than function in its split fashion. No matter how varied its guises of operation, and its metaphoric shifts, the cultural process only repeats itself. Culture never actually improves. Every "advance" is a trade-off bought at a price. The enthusiasms of novelty cloak the price momentarily, but not for long.

The semantic universe can be sustained only by enormous effort. Its gossamer web of illusion and fantasy is set up as a "permanent" island in a universal flow in which all moves. (Consciousness is an act, a movement, a process.) The great beehive activity of cultural "correctives" sustains and creates itself, and culture can never be stopped and changed out-there.

One can stop that world personally, by a shift of dominance within. Then it makes no difference what apparent madness is going on. For the flow can then complete its circuitry and work in this one case, and that is all that is important. Cultural thinking judges everything as a number's game, which keeps you contextually oriented.

13. Mind Engineering

Operation Bootstrap

In a world of truly blind people, how could the notion of "seeing" arise? Were the Naked Ape paradigms of our past scientism correct, none of our current "new-consciousness" ideas could materialize. Where blindness is a conditioned response, however, with the visual organs intact though inhibited, glimpses of light occur.

Among those discovering that blindness is not the natural human condition, an ordinary first reaction is "concern for all those poor people" who don't realize that blindness is not their natural condition. There is a desire to help others grasp the concept of nonblindness.

Our first reaction to recognizing a split within is to project and see the split out-there. Then we are drawn to heal that split out-there. Blind leading blind keeps the culture vital and "changing."

A splendid chap from a research "think-tank" came. Having been moved by reading *Crack,* he outlined an elaborate plan to "engineer" it into a commodity available and attractive to all the "lost souls" needing it, even if they didn't know of their need.

I asked him to consider our "reality-adjusted" mode of thinking as a saddled, bridled, riding horse, with the "autistic" mode, or the Primary Process, as the rider in that saddle.

Through acculturation, I pointed out, Horse is conditioned to selectively screen out that Rider. The Rider is silent, for one thing, guiding by the subtlest of motions on the reins. Horse, on the other hand, is a great talker. He talks to himself every minute he isn't talking to other horses. He is conditioned only to verbal commands, spoken and written. He amplifies his speech with loudspeaker systems giving his words an authoritative objectivity. And he keeps his vision riveted on word bulletins he has plastered everywhere, which concretize and mirror his speech. This word-world mediates between Horse's sense and percept, and he has no cognizance of having a rider.

Inevitably, though, some horse rushing around the track, tightly circumscribed by word bulletins and loudspeakers, will still occasionally get the odd notion that he is a saddle horse. Immediately, however, as he is conditioned to do, he projects this notion onto out-there. That is, he notices for the first time that his neighbor horse had indeed a saddle–*with no one in it*. (Understand, Horse sees only according to word labeling, and Rider is silent, without word label, and so is *non*cognizable.)

Enlightened horse then does a strange thing. He has an irresistible impulse, a great evangelistic passion, in fact, to jump into neighbor's saddle and grab those reins.

Periodically, then, we have these certain horses trying to mount the saddles of other horses. The maneuver is impossible, of course, since horse is simply not rider, and the saddle isn't empty at all.

Other horses note the folly of this attempt to get into neighbor's saddle. The problem, they report, is that no one can do this for another. It is a do-it-yourself maneuver. You must be your *own* rider. Evolution has brought you to this wonderful point where you can now get up there and *grab those reins yourself.*

These really sharp horses then offer (for a price) their system for doing nothing less than *getting you into your own saddle.* Such a maneuver is admittedly difficult. Exquisitely unique physical exercises, enormous outputs of energy, rigorous dieting, and careful tutelage are required.

Both systems take time, energy, money. The passion for new techniques keeps expanding awareness centers expanding, since each technique always finally fails. Each self-declared guide is continually stimulated as well, for if he could just get a *real* student, who would *do* right, perhaps the maneuver would actually work. This unmentionable qualification is something the students often suspect, but, like the congregation and the preacher, no one admits such doubt since that would dispel the hopes of all.*

So all these horses gallop around this arena on self-generated cues, while here and there some horses try to mount each other's saddles, while others twist about

* One day a crowd of little ruffians surrounded Nasrudin, the Mulla, teasing him and tossing pebbles. The Mulla cried out, "Boys, don't tease me and I'll tell you a wonderful surprise." "All right," answered the boys, "but no tricks, now." "Oh," exclaimed the Mulla, "the Sultan is giving a great banquet in his courtyard, open to everyone. Run quick and get some good things to eat."

Off the little boys ran. Watching them, Nasrudin suddenly gathered his robes about his shanks and rushed after them in panic. "Good heavens," he panted, "suppose it were really true!"

in wild acrobatics trying to get into their *own* saddle. Damnedest sight.

(Horse and rider are really what the American Indian thought the early Spanish cavalrymen were—all one creature. You can't have either without both automatically, and you can't have anything at all any other way.)

For a switch of metaphor and plagiarism (the horse metaphor was given me, the elaborations are mine) consider the allegory of The Cave. These men live in this cave where the shadows they cast on the wall are taken to be the real events. (This is the mirror-to-mirror function in the split mind.) All cognitive training is oriented to the shadows on the wall. Technologies and civilizations rise and fall around the proliferation of concepts concerning those shadows.

Occasionally, through poor conditioning (education is *so* faulty), some poorly acculturated (or just bored) soul breaks with his programming and *looks away* from the wall. Some, even, get a glimpse of the light coming from behind them, creating the shadows on the wall.

The light is blinding to one conditioned to look only at shadows, and the experience is numinus. The program breaker ponders this sign and weaves a conceptual scheme of *hope* for the cave-dweller. Beyond the cave is another, brighter and better life for all, when cave life is done. (Religion is the left hand of culture, as politics is the right.)

Occasionally a program breaker discovers the light source and finds that with this esoteric knowledge he can cast novel, unique, fantastic, nonordinary shadows on that wall. Immediately he is in great demand for his displays. He becomes a teacher, showing others how to alter their program and make novel shadows of their own.

A particularly strong figure is when a program director of the shadow world itself breaks program. He commands enormous prestige. The light and the new possibilities for shadowing are then interpreted within the framework of the wall-world technology. One then doesn't have to break program–the program is altered to include the new concepts of light, diffraction, shadowing, and all the ramifications. Without even turning the head one enjoys the fruits of progress.

There has been a persistent rumor, unfounded and easily dismissible, that there have been program breakers who glimpsed the source of light, turned around, and simply walked out that Crack. Nothing is heard of them, though, and the notion can be dismissed as fantasy.

Throughout my years of writing and rewriting *Crack*, my point of view seemed at odds with my social world. In the period after publication, however, I found a large "brotherhood" of compatible souls. I was introduced to sincere and brilliant research people who seemed on the threshold of "breaking through" into higher consciousness. It was an exciting time.

The breakthrough was to be an engineered coup. A host of enlightenment engineers were working on the modus operandi, however, and no consensus of problem or solution could be found. The approaches were as varied as the people involved and professional images were zealously promoted and guarded. Body disciplines headed the list, rigors of meditation, fasting, dancing, exercises, sensory overloading, breakup of body postures, altering consciousness, expanding awareness through biofeedback, and so on. Mind control would influence matter and maybe other people. Telepathic-clairvoyant powers, enhanced creativity, superlearning ability, link with the "higher cosmic forces" would lead to a sensory awareness sharpened to a semiorgasmic peak of permanent Maslow-high.

If one system opted for fasting, another went for superenergy. The greater the energy, the greater the consciousness. The higher the voltage, the closer to heaven. Massive protein intake, vitamins, and avoidance of down-syndrome food gave clear lines for action.

Or, biofeedback would rectify nature's failings. We would control every facet of the body, all those autonomous procedures heretofore left to primitive unconscious functions. We would take over the workings of the old-brain with our newer, better model. Control was sought over brain waves, glandular output, body heat, metabolism, pulse rate, oxygen consumption, assimilation, sleep cycles, and on and on.

Underneath all the activity was the longing for power. Power was suitably cloaked under a "new morality," of course, and would never be used for anything *bad*—for, above all, *ego,* that devilish imp within causing wars and poverty, would be abolished in the process, leaving only the pure, god-consciousness in control.

Prediction and control underlay all drives. One might even make the really big-time, right up to that seventh heaven where the whole cosmic show was run. And were one pure enough, ego-less enough, (or maybe of just plain hot enough mind voltage—who the hell argues with power?) one might even get his hands on the big computers themselves. Imagine! My God! (or rather—*ME*-God [you Jane].)

Here was operation bootstrap—a real do-it-yourself

scheme. For had not Evolution à la Bergson-Teilhard evolved us to this point of putting the trigger—or rather the *Light*—at our disposal? Was not ours the Great Commission? Surely we should not fail to carry the torch.

We assumed that through piling up nonordinary experiences, eventual powers would be generated by which we would work our way through the Crack—having generated that Crack in the first place. Thus there was an absorbing fascination to any and all reports of paranormal happenings. Somehow, just hearing about them from each other, or seeing the film of psychic events, seemed almost to create those steps in front of our eyes. A subculture jet-set emerged, rushing about the globe to witness the paranormal and report such to the waiting seminar-circuit.

In *Crack* I had used nonordinary phenomena, both personal and from the common domain, to show the arbitrary nature of the semantic reality. Somewhere along the way I lost sight of signs as signs and became dazzled, too, with sign production.

For instance, a study of brain-wave feedback unfolded a marvelous illusion. As you know, Alpha waves were thought to be the stuff of Zen and Satori, virtually god-think itself. Through biofeedback, one could achieve this age-old dream in a matter of easy weeks rather than the arduous years as in the old pre-technology dark ages.

Further, I read with fascination that Theta waves were recorded at the very moment of creative problem solving by mathematicians. From another study I found that infants spent much time in Theta and that it was believed that the foetus was in Theta *all the time*. Why, of course! "Unless you become again as little children . . . unless you be born again . ." Theta was the creative, prelogical mode. Learn to produce these waves, and biofeedback was the Way, and we would have control over the most elusive of all great human aspirations.

My synthesizing head-trip put together a composite of Sperry's split-brain research, Gurdjief, "body-knowing," Alexander, with a few adroit pinches of theological seasoning, into a fairly exciting and almost plausible "great-breakthrough" revival-circuit pitch. It went over quite well in campus lectures and weekend seminars. There we stood at the threshold of the Promised Land. And our great-hope syndromes, so carefully nurtured by our culture, fairly leaped for joy.

(Recently I ran into a long-standing national group organized along these lines. In their embarrassingly extravagant promises I recognized my own pitch, stripped of its intellectual trappings, and pared to a few bedrock tabloid naïvetés as presentably streamlined as a TV commercial. In a mere forty hours, and without any messy claptrap of equipment, you were promised ability to shift from Alpha to Theta to Phi Beta Kappa or Sigma Nu at the flick of a finger.)

My publisher-mentor, meanwhile, had scornfully dismissed my interests in "black-magic," and had made available to me several works on Taoism—that ancient, pre-Zen, pre-Buddhist form of Chinese thought. The significance of the Tao evaded me, however, until such time as I had run through enough of my new ace-up-the-sleeve activities to suspect their eternal bankruptcy. And I did bankrupt. My rationale ran dry. I could no longer kid myself about those next aces coming up, and in despair—without hope—turned my back to all I knew.

At that point my "path" abruptly changed. When the student is ready, the teacher appears. I found myself moving into areas in which none of my notions any longer held.

One "nonordinary" sign lets you know your current shell is an arbitrary construct. That's all signs are for. Any sign could, like the koan, shatter our facade of concepts. Any of the varied "techniques" don Juan tried on Carlos could have broken his circle. But, as I pointed out in *Crack,* there is an enormous force bending all lines back into the circle. I didn't know then that it was culture of which I spoke.

There is (was?) a well-funded group dedicated to the research into and discovery of *Force X*. Considered in the same class as atomic, gravitational, electrical, and chemical forces, *Force X* was considered that which levitates tables, carries the message in telepathy, "sends" the psyche in clairvoyant travel, heals in faith healings, and so on. The appeal was to organize scientists, parapsychologists, and research people into a great concerted drive to discover that *Force X*.

Tantalizing cases break out sporadically. Yuri Geller, for instance, does move objects, make clocks run backwards (or just disappear?) bends forks, crumbles nails, and so on, without touching them.

Only, he has no vague idea *how*. His brain-wave patterns show no change during his performance. All working with him are convinced (or were the last I heard) that they are on the "threshold" of a great breakthrough.[1] Force X will yet fall to prediction and control. Then, presumably, all of us will learn to move objects, disappear them, break forks, split diamond rings, and so on, just by our intent. The panacea of all our problems.

This great-breakthrough hope was expressed in the same way through the nonordinary happenings of Arigo, a Brazilaian peasant faith healer. Arigo had gone into profound trance one day and from then on was guided by a "doctor" speaking to him in his left ear. Following the doctor's advice, Arigo did absolutely unbelievable healings in unbelievable ways. For seven years Arigo administered to the poor and needy, never accepting anything for his services. He supported himself by day labor as usual, for four or five hours a day, and devoted ten to twelve hours daily healing the poor. He treated an estimated million and a half patients.

They lined up by the thousands wherever he went. He spent an average of thirty seconds per patient. To diagnose them he had only to listen to his guide in his left ear, and follow instructions. If an operation was called for, he whipped out his pocket knife there on the street corner and in one swift movement would open a chest, "repair" a cardiac disability, the chest closed, scar tissue formed, the patient moved on, the next moved up. For a displaced cornea, out came the knife, into the eye, the cornea was back in place. A tumor, out came the knife, the tumor fell to the pavement.

Researchers were naturally ecstatic over this breakthrough. A medical team went to Brazil with mobile equipment. They made their own diagnoses of sample groups awaiting treatment, compared notes with Arigo's diagnoses, treatments, and results. They found him infallible. The tumors were malignant, the cardiac conditions had been arrested, and so on. Wired up to EEG, however, Arigo showed absolutely no change in brain-wave pattern while performing his healing, and his gift seemed as much an unknown to him as to those investigating.

Seven years after beginning this ministry, Arigo was killed by an automobile, an event he had calmly foretold. The excited researchers were left with an impressive array of statistics, film, notes, great hopes, and complete bafflement. Buried with Arigo were his gifts and secret, leaving behind only mystery and frustration.[2]

This cycle is run through time and again. New performers are discovered in odd places on the globe and processed to no avail. The ace-up-the-sleeve syndrome blinds us to acceptancy of the great gift even when baldly presented. Prediction and control blind us to the fact that that which we so passionately seek already is, in the only way it can be, and in the Flow of things. Oh, no, we say in tape-looped unison, somewhere we have just slipped. Better controls and analysis, and that Force X will come into our hands, and then, surely, we will come into our own.

14. Playful Spirit

There is a quixotic, teasing element in paranormal phenomena similar to the "poltergeist" or playful spirit event.

In *Crack* I summarized parts of Leonard Fineberg's report of fire-walking in Ceylon. I did not include Fineberg's report of the aftermath of that strange night. It is apropos here and worth relating.

Among the European contingent present at the fire-walking there in Kataragama's temple yard, was a solid, reality-adjusted British lady of pronounced practicality. All that they had witnessed, she proclaimed, was trickery or illusion. No fire-walking had taken place and the nonsense about a local god, Kataragama, was native superstition. Her protests ran overly long as they all got into their cars for the drive back to the city.

It was a lovely, sunny morning as they set out, caravan style, along the single-track dirt road. Suddenly an enormous downpour of rain fell without warning, but only on the single car driven by the critical English lady. Immediately her part of the road was a quagmire and she veered off the track into the ditch. As suddenly the rain stopped, the sun shining serenely. The other drivers, untouched, leaped out and with joint effort got the car back on the road, the no-nonsense driver apparently unhurt. A medical checkup on their return showed no damage except that she had, right on her behind, in the conventional spot for correctives, a large black bruise, the shape of a hand. The god, Kataragama, as any of his followers will tell you, is a good-natured, whimsical god, but absolutely powerful within his small domain.

In the early 1930's, when Black Elk, the Sioux holy man, was very old, he asked his white biographer, Neihardt, to drive him back to his boyhood camping grounds at the head of the Badlands, where his first great vision had been given him. There the old man prayed to his grandfathers for forgiveness. He had failed, he felt, to sustain the faith and cohesiveness of his people through their conquest by the whites.

Black Elk prayed for a sign, a token of divine acceptance of him in spite of his shortcomings.

They were in the middle of an extensive drought, Neihardt reported, and a dry, cloudless day it was. After a long time of the old man's steadfast prayer, a mist formed about the group. Finally a thin, steady rain fell on them, and Black Elk wept with joy.

(Before linking this activity with poltergeists, imagine the research team–foundation money surely forthcoming–wiring Black Elk for EEG plotting of his brain-waves, asking him to kindly perform in a Faraday cage, tracing out every contingency, hoping to find that Force X that we might direct rainfall to needy spots in the dust bowl, put out forest fires or Watts riots, etc. Recall that don Juan pledged Carlos never to reveal his, don Juan's whereabouts, for some strange reason.)

The world is, as don Juan insists, a very mysterious place. We encapsulate ourselves in an equally strange shell of sameness, but we rob only ourselves, not the world. The "playful spirit" phenomenon occurs frequently in all countries and follows certain patterns. The activities are "paranormal" with objects appearing and disappearing; levitation is frequent; there is occasional light damage and small fires; loud noises are frequent. Mostly the activity is in the form of playful, whimsical tricks.

Poltergeist activity is nearly always associated with a pre-, or early, adolescent boy or girl, and particularly one having severe difficulty with reality adjustment. There are exceptions, but this is the pattern. In the early sixties a poltergeist occurred in Clayton, California, a tiny hamlet just outside Walnut Creek. A Mexican boy of thirteen, abandoned by his parents, was living with his grandmother when the activity began. Graduate physics students came from Berkeley, complete with infra-red film, recording devices, and equipment to "expose the fraud." (The editor of the local Walnut Creek paper was on hand, and the source of my account.)

Loud explosions occurred in the middle of the room where they sat, late into the night, long after the boy involved was asleep. No concussion was felt from these noises, nor was there any detectable source. Objects moved about and were attributed to earth tremor. Finally, after a quiet spell, a plaster madonna from the family shrine in the corner rose gently into the air, moved to the center of the room and hung suspended there. No hidden devices were detected.

In the fifties, the family of a young Irish girl of 12 moved to Glasgow looking for work. Left behind were the girl's pet dog and all her friends. Lost in the strange new land–they hadn't even a yard–she grew morose, silent, and withdrawn. There then began a poltergeist activity of remarkable duration and intensity.

Several researchers arrived and spent time in the crowded home. The activity grew more intense after the girl went to bed in the evening. The activity then centered around her bedroom. The standard ripping off of the bedclothes and the bed moving off the floor were followed by the lid of a linen chest starting to bang up and down. Unable to hold the lid down, several of the men sat on it, and it lifted them easily without pause, continuing to bang away without damage to lid, chest, or men.

Poltergeist activities would fill volumes. I have given

this brief survey to relate the activity to other paranormal phenomena, and to suggest the origin of all this activity to be in the "shadow side" of mind. "Autistic" seems to fit the poltergeist well since there is a childish, playful element in it.

Consider that the most crucial point in our "reality adjustment" occurs at puberty. At this stage, as Piaget outlined, logical development firms up, and the last vestiges of childhood autisms fade. Hilgard of Stanford found that the average person loses a certain flexibility of mind at this point. Cultural logic takes over at this stage, and dependence on the cultural context becomes complete. Peer-group reliance extends and the drive for authenticity and identity begins.

Identity, or placement of self in a stable context, is at stake. Until genital sexuality the preadolescent is not quite male or female. With development of genital sexuality, the "subdominant" gender splits off from the developing socially oriented ego. This follows the transfer of language to the major hemisphere of brain. The semantic universe with its constricting logic is taking over. Roof-brain chatter begins to crowd out the "still small voice." The self is being decentralized, thrown eccentric, giving over to a semantic context outside itself. The mute, creative mind, the connecting link with the life flow, is losing out, being damped down.

The reality adjustment of the preadolescent is always rough. Should it get extremely rocky at this point, if the rewards of reality modification do not offset the uncertainties of decentralization, and if the autonomous inner life maintains strong connections within the total mind system, then the ordinary cultural dominance system of mind may get out of phase. At that point there may be physical displays similar to the psychic displays of delerium tremens.

In delerium tremens, the alcoholic's waking and dreaming stages of mind get out of phase. Ordinarily our sleep and wake stages act by mutual inhibition, and on a fairly regular cycle. Alcohol in quantity prevents those sleep cycles in which dreaming occurs. The mind's need for dreaming grows intense, and since the alcoholic is never quite asleep or awake, the ordinary balance goes haywire. Dream sequencing starts firing in on "ordinary reality." The two modalities get mixed in the cognitive system. Waking nightmare results.

In poltergeist activity the mind dominance gets out of social phase. Then reality sequences may occur as shaped in the nonverbal mode of mind. *Crack* readers will recall my descriptions of "autistic phenomena" being nonlogical and not restricted to cause-effect sequencing. Once the restrictive activity of semantic-cultural logic is bypassed, the possibilities are not restricted to causal sequencing. Then reversibility thinking can structure events.

This continuum of possibility nevertheless must translate selectively, even in poltergeist activity. There is no being except in a mode of being. Just as the Zen Masters "intervention in the ontological constructs" remain outwardly selective according to his tradition and discipline, so is the poltergeist activity subject to the limitations of translation.

Translation by what or whom? This question is similar to the one concerning transference of the geometric drawings from my perceiving to that of my friends. In the Mexican boy's case, the possibilities were selectively "translated" by the boy involved. That is, what would occur to the imagination of a young boy when all possibilities are equal? For that boy's "playful spirit" is an aspect of that boy, just as the tangible "reality-adjusted" personality is an aspect of his less communicative side that has somehow broken out in "playful spirit."

Separation does not exist for that silent aspect of mind. The poltergeist, and other paranormal events of spontaneous sort, might represent a psychic frustration. Our ignored processes tug at us saying, in effect, "look it doesn't have to be the way you think it is."

The nonordinary is an expression of nonseparation. At some point there is no distinction between the Mexican child, figurine, and the gravity holding things to a relatable space. One can, suspending criteria, entertain any possibility in a continuum of possibility as being equal to any other possibility. The poltergeist is propositional logic at its most open, but out of phase. Don Juan represents such possibility "in phase" with his ordinary modes of mind.

The poltergeist activity might well be a "sign" for us. It may be that the individual's inner self, connected with the life flow, protests the constricting sentence being placed upon the unfolding life.

The performance occurs occasionally in adults. Carl Jung related such an incident in his memoirs. He and Freud were involved in a heated debate concerning paranormal phenomena. Freud had ruled such out, and was disturbed by Jung's interests. They were sitting in Freud's study, and as the afternoon wore on, Freud grew agitated over the uncanny nature of Jung's talk. Suddenly Jung felt a band of heat about his midriff, a tight tension.* Immediately there was a loud explosion—without concussion—in the area of the

* A similar physical sensation preceded Robert Monroe's out-of-the-body discovery.

bookcase. Both men leaped up, startled, and looked for damage or cause. Finding none, they settled down to their discussion again.

Jung realized that they had been given a "sign" of the very phenomena in question. This observation caused sincere agitation in Freud who demanded the conversation be dropped. Again, though, Jung felt the broad band of tight heat about his middle, and called out to Freud that another demonstration was in the offing. Sure enough, another loud explosion followed immediately, terminating the discussion and lending to the rift between the two men.

The principles of the world surely tend toward order, an order rather upset by the impish qualities of the poltergeist. And yet such events suggest a relationship for reality different from those we hold. The phenomena displayed by a Geller, Arigo, or Edgar Cayce might well be a unique gift occurring regularly within the larger body of man, and for our well being. These gifts are seldom discovered, and even then never unfold because there is no milieu for their flowering. They are seed dropped in shallow soil. Such gifts are not accepted and opened to, but are capitalized on by those who desire to duplicate the phenomena and incorporate it into the cultural circle of prediction and control.

The longing for black magic, levitation, telepathy, moving objects by thinking is a surface projection of a very genuine longing and need within. The need is for unity with the Flow. And, paradoxically, as poltergeist activity shows, the longing for magic is correct in a wrong way. "Paranormal" phenomena does express a connection between all things, an avenue beyond our constricting cultural conditioning.

The desire for justification of self in the social

sense is just as strong if not stronger, however, and shifts our desire for the flow back into cultural circles. (I will only mention Carlos's selective blindness caused by his desire for academic acceptability. Once he achieved such acceptability, his old grid disappeared and he saw don Juan in a new light.) Even those who dismiss the black magic aspect and are motivated only by "spiritual" interests are all too often only seeking a more unassailable form of ego-image verification, one less vulnerable to common criteria.

The issue is in *doing* or *not-doing,* in don Juan's sense. There is a difference between a sorcerer and a Man of Knowledge, between a Simon Magus and a Jesus.

Zen is clearly a form of not-doing. The clearest exposition of this was given by Eugen Herrigel in a short little work from the 1930's entitled *Zen in the Art of Archery.* Within Zen are several different disciplines or paths for following.* One of these is archery. This aspect of Zen bears resemblance to don Juan's surrender to "body-knowing."

Herrigel spent six frustrating years in Zen archery when he was a visiting professor at the University of Tokyo. Zen archery is a vehicle to get the student beyond the constrictions of his cultural orientation.

---

* Japanese Zen operates on two levels: the Zen Master of such rigorous physical disciplines as archery and swordsmanship, and whose mode of reality interaction is at a distinct discontinuity with the ordinary; and the equivalent of a "Zen Minister" who functions culturally, serving the emotional needs of ordinary people. A corresponding analogy might be in a great Christian mystic, and an ordinary "preacher" or "priest" who acts as counselor and guide for troubled souls. The technique of the ministerial type Zen is generally meditation, a form of "prayer" without content. This can be highly beneficial for those in the mechanics of daily life. Zen in the West tends to be of this "ministerial" type; I have met many who practice "just sitting," and benefit. I have met no one who has devoted years to a routine such as Herrigel's.

This was difficult for a Japanese, and virtually impossible for a westerner.

In Zen-archery, all notions of doing, force, space-time, cause-effect, subject-object must be somehow bypassed. The bow used is of ancient design and difficult to draw. The position assumed for holding and drawing, above the head, robs the arms of leverage, making the drawing even more difficult.

The Master draws the bow with no discernible effort. His muscles and tendons remain relaxed and unflexed. His breath carries the tension, for only in his "being breathed" is the maneuver possible. "It" draws the bow, looses the arrow, and strikes the target. The discipline is to learn *not to do any of that,* but to concentrate only on being breathed.

The frustration this causes a western orientation of cause-effect finds comparison only in Don Juan's trying to get Carlos to race through the desert in the dark by a trust in "body-knowing."

The Zen master can hit the bullseye at the standard sixty paces, without looking at arrow or target, in the dark or in the light. He stands with half-closed eyes in something suggestive of a trance stare, looking off into distant space, waiting for "It" to breathe him.

One night, for Herrigel's benefit, the Zen Master stood in the dark and put an arrow directly into the center of the target. He then proceeded to put a second arrow directly through the first arrow, neatly splitting its shaft, lest Herrigel think the first a coincidence.

Herrigel used the term "not-doing," and that was the issue. To not-do is to let "It" breathe you. Then "It" draws the bow, and at the "point of highest tension" looses the bow. The tension is in one's breath.

Finally, "It" strikes the target without the "doing" of one's aiming.

Through "It" breathing one, there is no subject-person drawing the object-bow and loosening the object-arrow to hit the object-target. There is only the event of "It" breathing one. Within this unified event there is only the "beingness" of the components of that unit. The mode of mind that automatically divides, fragments, and then tries to reunite is no longer dominant in the organism at that moment. The ordinary intellect is totally involved with the breathing by "It." This allows "It" to take over the organism. Firewalking involves a narrow, specific application of this function on a temporary basis.

Should the archery student hit an impenetrable "plateau" in his learning, the Master might use the student's bow for a time or two. The bow will then momentarily respond for the student as it did for the Master. Occasionally this can shake the student from his fixation.

I recall watching in semidisbelief as my New England dowser walked along, his forked stick leaping about in his hands, pointing direction and going straight down at the water-spot. The dowser suggested I cut a stick and try, which I did with absolutely no results. So he took *my* forked stick and I took his. For some forty-five seconds or so his stick twisted in my hand like a thing alive, utterly astonishing me. When its life faded, the dowser handed me the stick I had cut, to no avail, but with which he had been dowsing in the meanwhile. And it, too, was a live thing in my hand for a time. I could not hold it and prevent it from dipping down at some spot. The dowser had given it his power.

The purpose of archery in Zen is to learn to let

"It" breathe you. Under this dominance shift a different reality interaction unfolds. In our current enthusiasms the emphasis would get shifted to the wonders of nonordinary hitting of the target. "It" breathing one would not be the real issue, but "look how uniquely I can breathe." Zen-in-the-West tends to fall into the "ace-up-the-sleeve" category. Our passion is for "techniques," of just anything novel. Subcultures are forming to create mutual back-scratch, high feedback. "Satori" is equated with "feeling good," and high feedback. I'm OK, you're OK. I'll call you God if you'll call me God. We will converse each other up a numerical Jacob's Ladder, past God himself.

Our infinite capacity for rationalization cloaks our double-mindedness. And our cocreative function of mind will, with persistence, produce a new, startling, and self-fulfilling sort of temporary subjective state that seems to warrant the venture, for a time. We seize on a desired end as a set of expectancy that we hold with passionate intensity until that set acts as a temporary mediant between sense and percept, and we undergo a simulation of that expected. But nothing changes in our conditioning.

"Heightened awareness" or "expanded consciousness" is not "It" breathing you. Great experiences can be forms of ego enhancement. They can be powerful since they fill our drive for self-justification and ego verification. They can be buffers to despair. Esoteric buffers are sought by those to whom the common buffer is no longer effective.

In every western (and probably a lot of eastern) attempts along this line, the rational process never relinquishes dominance, for it can't. All our intellect can do is reprogram itself by dressing up the old programs, giving apparent novelty. We produce "tradeoffs" of a kind of Freudian-sublimation nature. We try to trick our sensory perceptual system into compliance with a set of expectancies promising enhancement of ego self. Expectancies can act as mediant for a simulation of effect. This is not to say that such enhancements are not "good," only to say that this activity has nothing to do with our Primary Process, and "It" breathing one.

One finds his level, I suppose, and that is as it should be. Few people really wish for the unity of "It" breathing them and "not-doing." They wish entertainment and diversion. As one form of diversion wears thin, others are always forthcoming.

My concerns are with that *Crack,* and nothing less. It was a surprise to find that the Crack forms in parallel with our "cultural egg," and is always there. Both of these phenomena began formation around age six, as Reversibility Thinking became functional. And to that capacity of mind I will turn again, before closing.

15. Reversibility Thinking

Our life unfolded from our parent ambient according to a logical plan. Object-constancy extended our intellectual grasp to reality out there, and opened the stage called childhood. Throughout childhood we knew an unbroken unity with reality. We accepted our given without question, and interacted freely with the world.

Operational thinking grew steadily as the ability to combine the possibilities from our interactions with reality, and enter into creative synthesis with our data. Doubt split our mind, however, closed this logical openness, and locked us into a word-built world.

Let me repeat here what Piaget calls the highest form of operational thinking: the ability to hypothetically consider any state along a continuum of possibility as potentially equal to any other state, and return to the same state from which the operation began.

We can use combinational forms verbally, symbolically, or mathematically. Through acculturation we use a verbal logic that is both subjective and ambiguous yet presumes to be objective and outer-directed. This verbal logic is almost universally employed since it serves the cultural function.

Language and logic were separate developments until around our sixth year. We developed our capacity for logical thinking through actual interaction with reality. This reality included the social semantic, but this was not decisively divisive until around six.

After age six we were capable of "considering any state as potentially equal to any other," and no longer accepted the given without question. This was a logical phase of our development.

In Piaget's definition for Reversibility Thinking we can read a definition of our Primary Program for our moment-by-moment interaction with reality, and our overarching plan for life.

Piaget lamented the scarcity of mature logic. "Pure" logic doesn't mature beyond our sixth year (or thereabouts) when the parallel metaprogram of culture begins to assume dominance.

Consider again that our brain seems divided according to function. Our language almost surely takes place in a different hemisphere of the brain than does the symbolic, creative thinking. Language no doubt shifted to the "logical" mode as it began to be used for cultural logic rather than just communication or expression. The procedures for logical sequencing are fragmented and meaningless, however, without the holistic activities of the nonverbal activities of mind. Mature operational thinking can only occur through an uncluttered interaction between the two modalities of thinking. But an "uncluttered interaction" is always made difficult at best and generally quite impossible through acculturation.

Only by "nonambiguous" thinking can the breach between the modes of thinking be bridged from our social-ego "side." Mathematics seems one such bridge giving results within its own space. Unbending intent is another, which can open one's personal interactions with reality.

Somewhere after our sixth year we had to adopt the semantic universe in place of a real one, and by adolescence the cultural metaprogram had assumed complete dominance. Our nonverbal mode, untrammelled with cultural constrictions, became noncognizant to our semantic orientation. But this nonconditioned modality continued to develop in our organism just as naturally programmed. Its very nonverbal character kept it intact from the fragmentations of a semantic structure.

It was impossible for this primary program not to develop so long as our organism developed at all. This Primary Program paralleled the growth of our semantic ego. Incapable of being warped by the fear of a hostile universe, this modality retrained its original communion-state character.

(Don Juan gave extensive instructions for "controlled dreaming," directives for which are also found in ancient pre-Zen and Sufi writings. Robert Monroe's strange *"Journeys Out of the Body"* are almost surely his representations of a similar function. The whole phenomenon can be considered within the "minor mode" activity outlined here, and intriguing implications appear.)

All "paths of knowledge" are attempts to open to this other modality of mind. Most paths recognize this modality to be already fully developed and only waiting to "breathe" one. It is not just fortuitous that the minor mode seems to be connected with "old brain" and autonomous activities and the noncerebral forms of "body-knowing." Many of the "body-discipline" paths try to approach union through gaining control of these "body-knowing" aspects. (It is interesting that Don Juan claimed he had nothing to do with keeping his body in superb shape except not to abuse it.)

Primary Processing and our Primary Program are not synonymous with nonordinary events or happenings. Our new "human-potentials" procedures do not remove the dominance of the acculturation process. Lives are still lived out in the pseudoreality of semantics. The world view of culture still functions as mediant. One may experience "highs" but he experiences as many "lows."

Neither don Juan nor the Zen Master experience "highs or lows." They are not "in a good space." They do not have a technique for producing good feedback. They do not run up and down a Jacob's Ladder of god-consciousness. There is no number system grading how much Primary Processing our "super-awareness" has produced.

The metaphors of meta-metaprogramming betray the cultural bias. Inevitably, after experiencing a "high" breakthrough, the new-consciousness devotee rushes back to report his experience to his subculture context. Thereby he betrays his underlying intent—which is social verification and enhancement of his image-of-self.

No moral failure is implied in this observation. (Only self-observation.) For this is specifically what our metaprogram programs us to do. Our metaprogram also programs our infinite capacity for rationalization to cloak this maneuver, thereby keeping us safely ensconced within the cultural circle, wearing a new robe of esoteria.

(The person who has shifted to Primary Process dominance is immediately, of choice and necessity, an anonymous person.)

Nothing can be willfully developed except the social ego-image. Nothing in the Primary Program needs to be developed—it already is. Our fantastic capacity for operational thinking is not a device by which we are to "evolve" ourselves. These capacities for creative interaction are the end products of processes over which we have nothing to do. We are that—we are already there.

There are many possibilities for mind's inventions through operational thinking. The highest forms can be subjective but "mature," as in art, religion, and ritual. Or they can be objective and outer-directed as in science or symbolic logic. Acculturation subverts but never destroys creativity. Art and science continually break free of the bondage of culture even as they are as quickly subordinated.

The issue in this book concerns an operational logic that is itself the "pattern" for transactive thinking. For there is a nonsymbolic form of operational thinking that is equally subjective and objective. This is a way by which one's actual life can be an art form or a scientific experiment. Reality interaction can take place free of all cultural mediations.

Reversibility Thinking can serve as one's conceptual pattern for grouping reality data into events. One's own personal life can enter into a continuum of possibility. Any state of your own being is then in a continuum of possibility for being, all held as potentially equal. And you can hold to a "return" to the same state, more or less, from which you began. You can overtly act out bodily in reality data, instead of thinking out internally in a metareality of representation, for employment of Reversibility Thinking.

Culture is a semantic mediant acting as proxy-for-reality interaction. The proxy alleviates direct confrontation with a "hostile" potential. Our homeostatic drive orients toward the "sameness" of the semantic mediant. All forms of intellect are incorporated into this drive to stay in familiar patterns, and interruption is a threat to survival.

Contrast this primary instinct with our "mature" operations of intellect, as in Reversibility Thinking. Reality is then a continuum of combination possibility which, by definition, is nonpredictable and noncontrollable. Were the end result "known" it would be a part of the known and familiar, a contradiction of terms.

Do you not see the tension inevitable between the logical movements of mind? Is there not a tension that involves our most formative survival mechanisms? Is it so puzzling that mature logic is seldom found or that semantic mediants are used for controlling and channeling the nonpredictable possibilities of the mature mind?

Do you see that flying to the moon in a machine is a satisfactory cultural maneuver while don Juan's claim to fly as a crow threatens our world view? Do you not see why alcohol, in spite of its poison and harm, is culturally acceptable as a buffer to despair, while we unleash a savagely instinctive reaction to psychedelics?

Homeostasis moves for a minimum of ambiguity. The dynamism might be said to operate on the simplest of either-or principles, growing from the simple choice of "flight-fight." That we end in the extreme ambiguities of the semantic reality and so in chronic anxiety is simple irony.

Reversibility Thinking opens to a continuum of possibility but returns to the "point of departure." An Einstein can hypothetically consider any state along a continuum, freely abandoning the stable sameness of, say, a Newtonian construct. Yet he arrives at the end in as predictable, controllable a unity as that left. He "returns safely." His unity then embraces a vastly larger potential, however. He has cracked and opened to us a larger egg. The "metaphoric mutations" afforded by his symbolic journey are what this aspect of operational thinking is all about. (The fact that the beauty of the operation is marred by the cultural application is beside the point right here, though it is a very large issue in its own right.)

A semantic reality operates in two ways: the generating of symbols within, projected onto data as out-there; and conceptual patterns that organize the out-there data to give the desired social percept. The two form a circularity of effect. The projection enters as data accepted as out-there. The intellect is then interacting with that which includes *its own projections*. Further, the intellect can only interact through a pattern of movement, or a concept, and that pattern is the cultural concept. Cultural data is shaped into percepts through the mediation of culture in a double-bind of circular definition.

Reversibility Thinking can itself be the "concept" mediating between sense and percept. The logical maneuver can be the way intellect interacts with data from out-there, and the pattern by which that data is conceived as a whole event. This action can give a world of data possibility without language and cultural concept as mediant.

What would happen were the pattern by which the intellect shaped its data "operational" as in Reversibility Thinking? The transactional movement of interaction would simply be "openness." We would then move along a continuum of possibility considering any state potentially equal to any other.

Einstein's intellect moved in a hypothetical continuum, but don Juan as a *person* moves in such a continuum. The continuum for movement is wherever he happens to be. Thus his desert is a marvelous world of equally conscious and equally interacting otherness. Don Juan is a point of self-conscious awareness in the Flow. To do this one can't use an intervening mediant standing as proxy for one's life or proxy for the data to be interacted with. Do you not see why the concept of a hostile universe makes this maneuver impossible?

In Reversibility Thinking there can be a return to a primal kind of sensory-motor act giving a percept without mediant. But only by a "childlike acceptancy of the given without question." It is in just this way that don Juan, Jesus, or the Zen Master utilize the most mature forms of developed logic in a "childlike" way.

Our cultural conditioning has built into us the parochial conviction that intellect and logic only develop by our schooling techniques. Hans Furth, from his ten years work with congenitally deaf children, claims that conceptual thinking develops through living contact with the environment regardless of the presence or absence of a "ready-made linguistic system."

Our extensive educational procedures train us not to interact with reality, but to sustain the cultural construct. Now we see why don Juan was scornful of Carlos's "concern" for the poor waifs denied the "benefits" and privilege of culture. The semantic reality acts as a mediant but don Juan's interaction is with a world of life processes equally valid. The data he interacts with are data interacting with him. No concepts can be used for such interaction other than "reversibility," simply seeing what the possibilities of interaction at that point are. The "other," the datum interacted with, is as much a determinant in the resulting event as is don Juan. Don Juan's continuum of possibility is a world of things-in-flow, not a world of things-thought-about.

The greatness of operational thinking is in the end result. Einstein's venture grew from and reflected back into his culture. A mirroring is involved as I outlined in *Crack*. Similarly, don Juan's venture affords a reality created as much by the desert world through which he moves as by don Juan.

We have no way of knowing what joy and delight don Juan might hold for that very desert with which he interacts. (How do you know but every bird . . .)

The coyote with which Carlos interacted at the end of *Journey* might have known its own greatest fulfillment in just that encounter.

To the semantically conditioned, nonverbal things are nonthinking things and even nonconscious. In don Juan's interactions, all things are equally conscious, with life processes of their own. When one enters the ambient of the bush, the water hole, or the deer, one acknowledges the ambient as the rightful grounds of those creatures or things. When one grants the bush its authenticity and equality within the field of consciousness, there is an infinitely open interaction possible between.

The world of semantics would split the dynamism into a thinking subject and a dead or semi-alive object. No interaction would occur. Simply nothing would happen. The desert would be its usual "dull place." Reversibility Thinking, on the other hand, would not filter the data through the "known stable-sameness" of the world-label "bush." Reversibility Thinking would open to the continuum of possible combinations of man-and-bush. In this kind of interaction anything could happen. And to one able to use his operational thinking in this way, every facet of the world would offer exactly the same infinite openness for interaction.

Could there be any conceptual scheme further from the cultural thrust for prediction and control? Can you conceive of any greater tension than between the organism's drive for stable sameness and the intellectual drive moving toward the potentials of "reversibility"? Can you not see why the cultural function *must* parallel, imitate, and finally dominate this open possibility?

Operational thinking is only possible against the

backdrop of the stable sameness of object-constancy. For only as an event varies from the known identity is it a meaningful maneuver. This is the way our program unfolded in the beginning. Intellect grows by moving from the known to the unknown.

In object-constancy the object is granted realness by the intellect although not present to the senses. In the same way, the end of a reversibility transaction is the stable point of departure. The point of departure is carried hypothetically as the connecting pattern for the entire event. But the pattern carried in absentia doesn't enter as an element in the transformation and interactions to which one opens. It is the stable point making the available *contrasts* meaningful. (It was only as the Einsteinian points emerged in contrast with the Newtonian that they became significant.)

In a don Juan venture, the prospect of a "safe return" to the starting point has no more assurance than does an Einstein venture that the initial idea will be borne out. One only embarks on the journey with openness. Holding any conclusion, such as physical safety, would be to divide one's intent. Instantly one would have set up a mediant buffer to act as proxy for interaction. Accepting death as one of the elements in every issue is necessary to *live* in Reversibility Thinking.

The possibility of mediation in mature logic, as found in science, poetry, or art, opens to its own form of continuum and potential. The form chosen creates its own content. (This is one of the ways we can, as G. Spencer Brown suggested, define a space and then enter into that space.)

Don Juan's interaction is with "reality-as-itself," a cosmos of equally alive and equally interacting dynamisms. Don Juan interacts with data he does not create. (The notion of solipsism could only arise in a split mind.) And yet don Juan's interaction creates the event of his moving into relationship. The highest form of Reversibility Thinking can be creatively acting on data, or openly interacting with that data. The first is dynamic, but the second is interdynamism. Only by equality could the latter be operative. Acting-on is one-way, interacting-with is two-way and offers exactly twice the dynamic potential. Creatively acting-on can mutate or create new data. Interacting-with creates only the event of interaction. After the event, all is as it was. Nothing is changed.

Our interacting mind can enter and withdraw from semantic possibilities "all in the head." Don Juan's venture is subject to the variables created by his very interaction. The desert is a lively place in his presence. Interaction challenges the homeostatic inertia. Don Juan's path of breathless wonder continually changes as he moves into a flow of contingencies of which he has *no* foreknowledge and over which he has *no* prediction or control. All he has control over is his intent.

Unbending intent is don Juan's pattern for moving through potential. The point of return is wherever the operation happens to be. The beginning is in the end. This is living in the Flow. This is the "impeccable action," action without separation from the Flow.

Every facet of western metaphysical thought assumes that existence separates from "essence," the material from the spiritual, the action from the "purity" of nonaction. Don Juan and Jesus stand at the opposite end of the spectrum from the "spiritual ascetic" who moves to transcend all action, materiality, and potential. The ascetic desires a point of "essence" beyond existence. This intellectual abstraction is the final resting place of the homeostatic desire for stable sameness.

Don Juan or Jesus deny "essence" and abstraction. Both are moving points of interaction with potential, sensory perceptors without mediation shutting out what is freely given. No protection is needed by the whole mind. The house not divided against itself has no mediants. The mediant is the divider.

A don Juan venture indicates what our biological development could produce did acculturation not forestall it. An unbroken unfolding could move in a reversibility kind of way, embracing with childlike acceptancy the given without question.

Since the assumption of a hostile universe acts as the mediant in conditioned thinking, a prerequisite to don Juan's position is acceptancy of one's own death. Acceptance of death doesn't grant "hostility," to the universe—rather, it frees that universe from the fragmenting force of the death concept. There can be no neutral, childlike acceptance without acceptance of one's personal death. Don Juan's universe is, like the child's neither hostile nor friendly. It just *is,* an open continuum given for interaction. To be fully Man is to recognize the gift as given, and to accept and enter into this gift, without qualification. Nothing more is required.

16. Embracing Despair

The Acceptance of Death

In my early childhood world, plants, trees, and flowers were all alive. Everything was alive. Everything was an extension of my own awareness. Certain great trees had numinous qualities, to be approached with awe and discretion. I talked with violets and buttercups I picked, carefully explaining our "need" of them at home. Cresting the top of one particular wind-swept, sage-brush hill inevitably produced a strong sense of the uncanny, a breathless expectancy that the next instant I would move into another realm. Early dawn held an irrestible pull for me, a thin veil of separation and a longing, producing that "grape bursting in the throat."

The early morning song of the robin was compelling. Robin conveyed worlds of "knowing" needing no elucidation. For years after, robin calls were nostalgic, hinting at something lost yet near. As I grew older I would still get up at dawn, trying to get that elusive, nostalgic quality again.

Only recently did I find why, to mix metaphor,

there had seemed to descend a "glass darkly" over my hearing as I grew older. As a child I had listened to robin in absolute silence. My inner dialogue, or roof-brain activity, had not begun. I heard the world as I was not to again, and robin had been the knowing of unity and flow.

A primary perception in plants seems authenticated in the work of Cleve Backster, in spite of occultic misappropriations and academic scoffings.[1] The affinity with animals described by Carlos and Don Juan was antedated by several years in a slim little volume entitled: *Kinship with All Life.*[2] J. Allen Boone, a Hollywood writer, had a metanoia type of transformation through his relationship with a remarkable dog, Strongheart. The dog told Boone "All there was to know," in that knowing that requires no language.

Overt forms of Primary Processing are fascinating. We attempt to reproduce these in the hopes of gaining a foothold in such a reality, but a Primary Process is not the issue for us. Our specific, individual Primary Program is that for which we are made. Our actual life process is the issue. History, mankind, society, progress, evolution, cosmic principles, noospheres, biospheres and split hemispheres are all abstract expressions from culture.

Our Primary Program breaks through to us at times, in spite of us. We then function in our Primary Perceptions, momentarily, perhaps as a sign. Consider this account, kindly furnished by a *Crack* reader:[3]

> I was about 12 years old at the time and it happened on a long hike at summer camp. We had been walking for about three hours and I was tired and sweaty. I was climbing a path, looking at the ground. The sun was very hot.

Suddenly I felt as if scales had fallen from my eyes. The grass became intensely green, the pebbles on the path were shimmering with reality. I felt as if I had never truly seen the world before this moment.

It happened again some weeks later. This time I had completed an exhausting hike and couldn't wait to plunge into the cool lake. I ran down a path and dove in. The coolness and caress of the water was exquisite.

I came up from my dive and floated on my back. A mountain was in the distance. Sunlight reflections were dancing on the water. It was peaceful and beautiful. Then it happened . . . the scales seemed to drop as I lazily looked at the mountain. Again I had this shock of reality.

I cannot forget these experiences even though some 20 years have passed. What happened? The grass seemed to be me, the pebbles, too, and the mountain. No, not seemed. They *were* me. That's what made the effect so powerful. It was not a concept but direct experience, as unarguable as crunching into an apple. Something in me opened and for a split second I knew that I was That.

. . . My childhood was a forgetting . . . the fall into a cave of shadows . . . a spectacular misunderstanding. I must remember that I never lost what I thought I lost. . . .

Here is the whole self breaking through to say: "This is the way it is." But one drifts back. The world is too much with us.

In a group-awareness weekend we would "simulate" this experience. We would talk about "feeling," awareness, being-with, atonement. We would immerse ourselves in pool or creek under the tutelage of the group-guide intoning being-with, feelingness, "don't you just *feel* that?" We would examine the blade of grass, the stone, to the directing drone of feelingness and mystic unity—urging us to taste with our toes, hear with our navels, feel with our backsides.

We play our parodies over like our endless grinding of sex hoping to stumble on love.

We hunger for wholeness and express it on every hand. The scientist longs for a "field theory" to unify the fragments of his thought. Ultimate prediction and control are his dream. The theological equivalent expressed long ago as monotheism. The scientific form expresses as an insatiable appetite, an intellectual concupiscence desiring more than the very stars could ever assuage. (Is it thus they recede from us —the everlasting ace-up-the-sleeve?)

The spiritual passion for unity is an involuted concupiscence, a blotting out of the material and digesting inward to a primal point of ultimate safety. Or, having lost cognizance (if we ever had it) of our "ally at left hand," we project him out there as an ever more remote abstraction. We end with the monotheistic god of Hebrew and Greek, the abstract "Nobodaddy" abhorred by Blake, the "moral governor of the universe," an intellectual nightmare.

In Teilhard de Chardin's *Omega Point* we find the unhappy marriage of this proxy heaven and too real hell, the "reconciliation" of these scientific-theological opposites that prove functionally identical. The *Omega Point* makes divine virtue of cultural necessity; sanctions that cultural force splitting our minds from our eternal now, and granting us, in turn, sainthood for "pimping" for history. The intellect's desire for total dominance leads to the final abstraction. God is placed at the most remote "futuristic" hypothesis conceivable—the ultimate carrot is placed before the eternal donkey.

(Add to this the error I fell headlong into in *Crack,* of presuming to "seize control of the tiller of the world." Incrementally piling up ever newer, greater illusions of prediction and control, power on power, the dying dreams of a dying age were bedecked with religious pageantry.)

Consider, instead of monotheistic abstractions, and power plays for mad cultures, this uniquely human and personal account given by an Apinaye warrior of one of the Ge tribes of eastern Brazil:[4]

> I was hunting near the sources of the Botica Creek. All along the journey there I had been agitated and was constantly startled without knowing why.
>
> Suddenly I saw him standing under the drooping branches of a big steppe tree. He was standing there erect. His club was braced against the ground beside him, his hand he held on the hilt. He was tall and light skinned, and his hair nearly descended to the ground behind him. His whole body was painted and on the outer side of his legs were broad red stripes. His eyes were exactly like two stars. He was very handsome.
>
> I recognized at once that it was he. Then I lost all courage. My hair stood on end, and my knees were trembling. I put my gun aside, for I thought to myself that I should have to address him. But I could not utter a sound because he was looking at me unwaveringly. Then

I lowered my head in order to get hold of myself and stood thus for a long time. When I had grown somewhat calmer, I raised my head. He was still standing and looking at me. Then I pulled myself together and walked several steps toward him, then I could not go any farther for my knees gave way. I again remained standing for a long time. Then I lowered my head, and tried again to regain composure. When I raised my eyes again, he had already turned away and was slowly walking through the steppes.

Then I grew very sad.

Is this not toward which our consciousness yearns? The invitation therein was for union, which petrified the hunter as it would any of us. Culture is culture. And on the passing of that magical moment offering union, we, too, would be filled with sadness.

There is a vast difference between this God, whose eyes are like stars and whose hair nearly touches the ground, and the intellectual creation of the late Greeks and Hebrews. The Indian's God arose from the very earth, from the flesh and blood of life. The Indian's God meets man as man, silently, for all is already known there. Nothing needs to be said. The God is the Indian hunter himself, perfect, his Primary Program fulfilled, ever there awaiting union. "God is a *man,*" cried William Blake, "for, as a cup cannot conceive beyond its own capaciousness, man cannot conceive of anything greater than himself."

Jacob gave a similar glimpse, finding God to be "also here," in this place—wherever Jacob was. When this otherself appeared, Jacob wrestled him all night and thereby gained his "blessing," his power. Don Juan and don Genaro both met and wrestled their "ally" to win his blessing. The Apinaye warrior's God invited this divine confrontation. There is the reunion with our long-projected self; and then the split within is seen to be nonexistent as it always was. That silent other-self has unfolded in parallel, and according to plan, in spite of and unbeknownst.

Don Juan knows, as well, a host of "momentary deities." There is the god of the water hole, the water spirit who is that water hole. There is a spirit of the wind, for the god is that wind. (Don Juan would cognize Kataragama out of the very soil of Ceylon, were he there.) In a sanctified life, a centered life without split, everything is, like one's life, sacred. The god is everything, and yet everything is unique and individual.

Where everything is sacred, including one's life and self, nothing needs to be permanent, for there can be nothing *not* sacred. The sacred is all one thing, all one Flow. The Flow is the river which can't be stepped in twice. The God of the wind is never the same. Mescalito, God of the tiny cactus, is different each time, yet consistent.

There is no "essence" abstracted out of being. There is only being. Monotheism was an "essence" finally abstracted out of the very cosmos. Eastern metaphysics suffered a failure of nerve at the problem of being, and proposed to stop thinking and so remove the illusory world. They denied the creation its reality and meaning. The great gift is thereby turned down. This is hardly the same as don Juan's stopping the world semantically created in order to enter fully into the real one eternally being created. Eastern negation represents the final extremity of the split mind's intellectual abstraction.

Don Juan is God-who-is-don-Juan. He talks, though no words are needed, with the magical deer who is God-as-that-deer. Their "exchange" is the Flow interacting in that reality fashion. When Carlos opened to his whole mind he talked with the coyote who "knew about things." In this "knowing" there are no "facts," there is no "information," no words, just that which alleviates the great homesickness and longing by giving one "knowing."

Jesus knows a God who is "in him" as he is in the God. There is no abstract essence of monotheism here. Jesus's being is God-being-Jesus. To see Jesus was to see God, for the God has no other being than a "being-as-something."

Most of us know a longing and yearning beyond the cultural ace-up-the-sleeve. Any attempt to translate this yearning into a fulfillable action seems only to trigger the cultural conditioning into play. Any "doing" to respond to the yearning expresses itself, in the last analysis, as a move to enhance our cultural image of ourself–it translates as a bid for authenticity–just what we were programmed to bid for.

Classically this was recognized as the problem of action and inaction. All action seems to separate one from the flow since action is "doing" and we are culturally conditioned to do. All action reinforces the culture and our split. Various forms of denials, negations, and non-actions emerge as attempts to attain unity.

All being is a tension of form and content. To be fully human is to accept that tension. To be perfect is an esthetic feat. One must live his life as a work of art in which one balances form and content.

Our intellect sees that our form must die, and

doesn't want to play the game. Intellect tries to become its own form by denial of the body. The "priest" in our head splits sex from spirit and so creates culture. Surely in the Flow all forms are transient, since consciousness is an act, a movement. Spiritual paths of denial betray their genesis, they are expressions of the death concept.

The final victory of the death concept is in the "spiritual" denial of life.

Don Juan and the Zen of archery stress "not-doing." And yet both are strenuously active. Non-action is hardly the same as not-doing.

In Zen archery the Master himself must practice daily to maintain his balance. For inevitably, one practices his cultural condition at every hand, with every breath and word, spoken or read.

Don Juan practices his "openness to his spirit" every instant, with every act. He devotes exquisite care and attention to every detail of his life, for he is ultimately responsible. When he uses his acculturated mind, as he must in dealing with our irrationality, he knows exactly what he is doing.

Carlos's use of the word *impeccable* to describe don Juan's every move was hardly accidental. Look it up and you will find *impeccable* coming from the Latin *peccare,* to sin, To be *im*-peccable is to be without sin, without "separation from God." This is both heresy and nonsense to classical metaphysics and theology. Since our Greek Hebraic concepts considered God as "essence" abstracted out of all "impure existence," existence itself ended as a kind of primal sin.

The great discovery is that God and Culture are not synonymous.

You can't logically draw on those elements that

will "lead you" to your Primary Program. Your cultural intellect produces only itself. Culture replicates itself intact, just as object-constancy formed as a total effect. Just as in the reverse-goggle image experiment, you might try to turn your cultural view this way or that, but it is built into your very body and responds as a unit.

No schematic is available to the reasoning forces of mind for "bridging the gap," to the Primary Process. The history of man has been the attempt to do just that—for then we could gain control over and implement the functions of the Primary Process, making it subservient to the cultural passion for prediction and control.

This drive for control always appears perfectly logical though it always fails. It seems logical since the cultural mind is still an aspect of the creative function. I outlined this creative play in *Crack*. But a split mind can create only a split world.

The Primary Process can't "bridge the gap," either. There is, in this sense, no grace. For the Primary Process to heal the split is impossible, since the split *does not exist* save in the imagination of man's split mind. To the Flow all is unity; there is no split of anything. William Blake knew the dragon guarding the Tree of Life to be spun of man's imagination.

No "doing" on our part can ever get us out of our bind, and there is no "doing" anywhere else to "do" it for us. There remains, then, only this "not-doing" as outlined by Herrigel and Carlos. These paths are not available to us, though, (there are not many don Juans or Zen Masters in this world) and we can only look for pointers.

Not-doing is a turning. Doing is our culturally conditioned response, common-sense, rational, coherent, sensible response. Not-doing is a reversal, a turning upside down or inside out, a going through a mirror. William Blake said, "where you see white I see black."

Not-doing has to do with "not judging," for instance, but we immediately interpret this in a moral-ethical framework, which is cultural doing.

A "denial of self," is involved in not-doing, but we interpret this in a moral-ethical sense again, thinking of substituting altrusm for selfishness. Or there is the claim to abolish the ego, which would be like killing one's horse in the middle of a race.

Denial is not eradication, but a shift of dominance, the true turning. The issue is dominance in the organism. Who runs the show? The God or the pimp?

Don Juan's erasing of his past is not an abolishing of ego, but a refusal to pimp for his history. As Jesus leads his followers to be "in the world but not of it," don Juan leads Carlos to "see" in the Kingdom, or *look* in the world of folly, as the situation demands.

The whole man is wholly in this world. Ego is half the self. Culture conditions this aspect of being to *assume* dominance. The not-doing of repentance is a turning *from* this dominance program. It is the risk of self to an unknown and unknowable "empty category" unavailable for analysis, prediction, or control. The issue lies with the death concept.

Our self-system is a criteria system, and we have no switch for shutting it off. There can be no rooting out of our criteria. There can only be a turning and not-doing according *to* that criteria.

Single vision, purity of heart, or unbending intent, is acting *as* though one's metaprogram did not exist. Of course it *does* exist, and of course all evidence before you daily confirms that existence. Only unbending intent can hold you to a turning from that constant confirmation.

In both don Juan and Jesus, death lies as a key stratum. Acceptance of one's death suspends the cultural concept of death. Acceptance of death is a way of "agreeing quickly" with the great adversary. The death concept is sustained only by the energy of resistance it can generate.

The frustrations of a Herrigel or Carlos lay with conflicts between survival drives, not matters of "wilful disobedience" to some divine directives. To allow "It" to breathe you is to suspend your survival techniques.

Once confronted, without ambiguity or doublethink, the "cross" is found to be light. Death as personal is very much different from the cultural concept of death. Once accepted, death is an integral component of every event, as the left hand to the right.

The cultural death concept could only be instilled in a mind split off from its life flow. Only in a semantic web that separated everything into dead particles could the cultural concept of death even have originated. And that concept, of a death alienated from all life, creates a horror impossible for the mind to bear. The concept sends its recipient off into paroxysms of desperate search for buffers to insulate the self from that hideous idea. These buffers ever unfold to egg us on, and ever fail to assuage our despair.

One can't mind-zap his way into the Primary Process, but one can embrace his despair, for to be without hope is to accept your death. You can pin your life on a *longing*—which is not the same as hope. You can move in spite of conditioning and act-as-though–as though you were not afraid, as though you were whole, as though life were benevolent without qualification. And when your longing is greater than your programmed drive foı authenticity and survival, your teacher will appear.

Wrestling with one's death is a wrestling with one's self for dominance. And in this confrontation you may, Jacoblike, win from your death his blessing, as he wins from you your acceptance of him. At such acceptance of your death you not only find the dragon to be of paper, the cross to be light, but death to be an intimate, real, alive, vital, and moving force. Accept him unambiguously, and death *is cognized instantly,* with an enormous blow of recognition.

At that instant we realize the odd polarities of our thinking, the subtle hints of myth, poetry, physics; the "lefthandedness" of the subtle creative forces in nature; Bruner's "thinking for the left hand"; why the God Odin had to put out his right eye to drink of the spring of poetry and wisdom; why the Brazilian healer, Arigo, heard his guide in his left ear; why don Juan and Carlos saw their death at their left hand and found in him their confidant, advisor, friend, and source of power; why don Juan promised Carlos that he would *recognize* his ally, regain his memory of his ally (but you *know* who he is, don Juan insisted, you already know); why Jesus claimed to sit at the *right hand* of his Father.

One's moment of recognition is one's return to unity. Then one knows the other self, universal yet personal, to have been unfolding in its Primary Programming all along, in spite of the madness, in spite of the metaprogramming overlay. Frost's *Road not Taken* was taken, and the parallel lines merge in a single thrust.

Then and only then can we recognize the true role of our logical, semantic, cultural thinking; dominant no longer; no longer a murderous tyrant trying to devour the universe; but a responsive tool, responsive to a process far beyond the personal yet most intensely and completely one's true and final self.

For at that moment of recognition, that joyful recognizing and remembering of something that we have always known, that shock of *of-courseness!* that is the most profound of experiences, we recognize that God and Death are *identical*–our death there at "left-hand" is God himself.

Acceptance of our death brings the whole cultural charade crumbling to dust, and we understand why the cultural concept of death closed the door to life so conclusively–why our childhood and adolescence was such a "spectacular misunderstanding." Acceptance of our death creates our first tentative move toward life–a move which the Flow seems ever awaiting: for only at that point can God arc the gap of our being, and wake us to what we have always been –ushering us into this great and perfect gift, so freely given.

Notes

A note on my notes: References to my book, *The Crack in the Cosmic Egg,* are not itemized here. Only when specific reference to a work is needed have I credited a source other than listing the work in the bibliography. If only one work by an author is listed, only the name and page number will be cited. For the most part, these "notes" are additional material or peripheral arguments.

Chapter 1. *Stable-Sameness*

1. Whitehead. p. 49.
2. Sullivan. p. 168.
3. When we "project," we take an internally generated effect and put it "outside our self," placing its source as elsewhere. For instance, we "project" our weakness by seeing it in our neighbor, or our child. A child will project his fear onto imaginary sources outside. A scientist might "reject" an occultic account of "paranormal" phenomena, but the occultist generally "projects" the event, seeing it as evidence of powers-out-there.
4. Tart. "Physiological correlates of psi cognition."

5. *Mediant* means mediation, literally going-between. Language as a mediant device "explains," or interprets a source to a recipient. Cassirer wrote: "Language moves in the middle kingdom between the 'indefinite' and the 'infinite' it transforms the indeterminate into a determinate idea and then holds it within the sphere of finite determinations." (p. 81.) Colin Cherry writes that: "We do not perceive and know things as they are; we perceive signs, and from these signs make inferences and build up our mental models of the world." (1957, p. 262.) (Our signs and models are given us by culture, I might add. Our "model" of the world then *mediates* between our signs selected and our final product of perception.)

   Werner & Kaplan (1963) write that man "transforms his milieu into objects-to-be-known and orients his action primarily toward the cognitive objects *mediating* between him and his physical milieu." Furth refers to the mediating effect of the symbol. We symbolize that which is "known," and then see this as out-there.

   When Bruner referred to the mind as an "editorial hierarchy" determining which data to select and process, he refers to the *mediating* effect between sense and percept. Reference to a "semantic reality" recognizes the mediating effect of language.
6. Furth. p. 225 ff.
7. Furth. p. 200, 228, etc.
8. To assume that human thinking arises from language is a natural expression of the semantic bias that shapes our mind and reality. All thinking seems a direct product of speech and our

linguistically carried heritage of "knowing." To break from this assumption, as Furth did in his work with congenitally deaf children, is an example of what de Bono calls "lateral thinking." See again Whitehead's p. 49 comment.

9. Furth. p. 177
10. This "mirroring effect" was one of the principal notions in my book, *Crack*. The argument is too involved for summary.

Chapter 2. *Sensory-Mediant-Perception*

1. Myklebust relates how loss of one sense alters all senses. (p. 48.) Lack of one sense changes the structuring in synesthesia (the cross-indexing that takes place between all biological functions.) (p. 50.) For instance, when hearing is absent, other sensory equipment structures differently. The pre-verbal experience of the hearing child is different from the same chronological stage in the deaf child. (p. 60.) Since seeing is an overall biological act and "synesthetic," persons blind from birth and receiving "sight" through an operation later in life "see" only a chaos of color blotches. The experience seriously disrupts their ordinary sensing. In order to orient and reestablish spatial and tactile identity, such patients must close their eyes. The patient may reject the intruding disorientation by a kind of "hysterical blindness," reestablishing their homeostatic balance.

   To restructure their sensory world and conceptually build order into the visual chaos would be a chore of first magnitude, similar, perhaps, to Carlos's problem with don Juan.
2. *Concept* is a patterned *act* of intellect, a way

by which thinking moves to process reality data into whole events. Piaget points out that "Experience . . . is not reception but progressive action and construction." (1962 p. 365.) Conceptualizing is also "synesthesia," a cross-indexing of all sensory apparatus to the service of some schematic for patterning reality.

Furth (p. 225) points out that the concept can't be experienced, it *is* the experience.

3. Harry Stack Sullivan explored this infant rejection of anxiety back in the 1940's. Studies are continually rediscovering this hard fact. The "wet nurse" of past times existed for the well-to-do, who have traditionally been more up-tight over childbirth, nursing, and so on. While many mothers lose their milk with a first child, most prove capable of nursing the second one, being less tense, and so on.
4. Furth. p. 174 ff., 197.
5. Furth. p. 176 ff.
6. Furth. p. 177.
7. Furth points out (p. 180) that language acquistion is only one aspect of symbolic behavior. Language *is* a symbolic activity; symbolic activity is *not* an outgrowth of language. Word play becomes language only *after* object-constancy.
8. Piaget claims that "Intellectual organization merely extends biological organization." (1962 p. 409.) And biological interaction *must* be employed for the mind-body organism to grow in its biological extensions into reality. That is why schooling as now practiced is disastrous to creativity and intellectual growth.
9. While abstract conceptualization has been a *gradual* development since object-constancy, it opens

as a fully functional possibility around the sixth year. This marks the end of childhood. (See Furth p. 181.)

10. Bruner's observations concerning lack of operational abilities in preliterate cultures need qualification. The "civilized," western adolescent would not survive the Australian Aborigine's "walkabout" initiation experience, for instance, since his sensory-perceptual scheme would not process reality data in that survival manner. The Aborigine is using an advanced form of logical processing, just in ways unrelated to our abstractions. That the preliterate culture's child quickly adapts to our forms of propositional logic, as Bruner demonstrates, shows the enormous flexibility of intellect, not the superiority of our schematics. Would our schoolchildren, time-lined and sequenced into fragmentation, readily grasp the cultural logic of the Eskimo or the Aborigine? Furth and Piaget stand as correctives to the somewhat chauvenistic semantic assumptions on which Bruner stands.
11. Furth. p. 194.
12. Furth. p. 184.
13. Piaget's definition is quoted by Furth. p. 175.
14. If culture restricts Reversibility Thinking to "mutations of the Semantic Universe," don Juan and Jesus represent that modality as an interaction with reality itself. Most "paranormal" phenomena are occurrences of Reversibility Thinking. One of the issues of this book will be that this mode of operational thinking is a biological endowment by which our interactions with reality can be infinitely open and creative. So far we have only semantic or "occultic" channeling,

each of which is constricting. Don Juan and Jesus represent radical "lateral" departures.

15. I am using this limited reference to Geller's "fork-bending" trick only because I know of its authenticity. The age factor is what intrigues me most, that Geller was seven when starting on this journey, that most of those imitating him are over seven and under fourteen. This forces me to override my growing distaste for this whole area, a distaste brought about by the sensational "copout" performances of those reporting *on* Geller.

This problem needs a separate study–not on the nonordinary claims for Geller, which are generally in keeping with other phenomena, but on the serious misappropriations and psychological projections resorted to by both Geller and those working with him. I am speaking particularly about the embarrassingly naive projection onto "Extraterrestrial Forces," and such. It is understandable that Geller might make fantasy projections concerning his gift, since he has no vague idea how the phenomena occur. It is incomprehensible to me how trained, acute men could accept such projections.

The problem needs to be related to another current projection that is enjoying popularity, projecting "cosmic powers out-there" all the great achievements of our past civilizations. Archeological curiosities are attributed to "flying-saucer spacemen" of the past. I can only cry out *NO!* Stop this! We are looking at Man–Behold His Works. We have been on this marvelous globe for nearly three million years, rising and falling in wave after wave of greatness. Never underestimate what we may have done many times over.

Geller's peculiar gift is an example of Reversibility Thinking in reality interaction. Aspects of his ability are continually being found. Such ability is seldom accepted, but is projected out-there onto "cosmic powers," and divine visitations. Man has been projecting his "divinity" for eons to evade the awesome responsibilities implied therein. In Don Juan and Jesus we find acceptancy of this capacity—an open interaction with the "god within."

16. Let me emphasize that creating the cultural construct is a reaction the child is forced into making. No two semantic constructions can ever agree, as a result, since each is created by the unique self-system. This underlying lack of final consensus security keeps us continually anxious to verify our reality experience verbally. Were our interactions according to a Primary Process, such "identity," problems would not arise.

Chapter 3. *Prediction and Control*

1. Melzacks. See Bibliography.
2. *See* John C. Lilly's *The Center of the Cyclone,* The Julian Press, 1972.
3. *See* Lee, Dorothy, p. 144-5.

Chapter 4. *Feeding and Feedback*

1. Furth. p. 178-9.
2. Furth. p. 192-3.
3. Some idea of the child's "communion state" will be suggested in the final chapter of this book.

In erecting buffers to fear we erect barriers to the Flow. Don Juan represents the capability of a selective drawing on the Flow according to need.

Chapter 5. *Lying*

1. Colin Cherry wrote that our mental experience is that which is real, while matter is a mystery. (A return to Primary Processing reinstates the reality of *all* things, while opening to the mystery of interaction.) Furth points out (p. 172) that symbolic formation gives "knowing." Knowing in this sense is passive, an habitual homeostatic state, an act of intellect that is not active thinking. Thinking is then our "ongoing interaction" with a reality.
2. Harry Stack Sullivan spoke of the "as-if performance" of children.
3. "Internalizing speech" is a controversial subject. Vigotsky (1962) believed that speech was "phylogenetic" and that "thinking" develops separately from speech development. Speech and thinking serve different functions, and at a certain age intertwine.

   Luria Yudovich (1959 p. 20) asserts that overt speech dies out in the six or seven year old when such "oral reinforcement" is no longer needed. When the child can make on-the-spot simulations and self-regulations according to need, the tendency of overt speech is dropped. Bruner considers internalized speech a prerequisite for logical thinking. Transformations of internal speech equal transforming of outer experience. This seems qualified by Furth's recent studies and the general character of "internal speech" itself.

Vigotsky considers "inner speech" our ego thinking, and "outer speech" our social communication. He considers the phonetic aspect of speech "oral," the semantic aspect "internal."

All these observations and arguments enter into the function of internal speech, perhaps, though none is satisfactory of itself. The socialization aspect, as presented in this book, is the catalytic component acting on all the contingencies.

4. Myklebust (p. 116) felt that identification of self was fundamentally related to language acquisition. I would qualify this to say "identification of one's *social image* of self, or social ego" is so oriented. The self-system of the young child, still within the communion state "Flow" of life, is not language based. *Also see* Furth p. 192 ff.

Chapter 8. *Will to Power*

1. Denial of *beingness* occurs in all cultures. For instance, anthropologists took film of a New Guinea tribe isolated for some five thousand years. (See *under the Mountain Wall,* five seasons in a stone-age culture.) The film clearly shows the "peer-group" effect operating in the "warriors," each out to try to "prove himself" in the eyes of the others.

   The American Indian culture was extraordinarily cruel, largely because of the need for each young man to "prove himself" in the eyes of a kind of historical criteria. The young man underwent extreme suffering in his attempt to "prove himself worthy" to the god. Each tribe slaughtered the other not so much in "territorial" disputes as in their unceasing need to win peer-group acceptancy. There are no cultures that operate outside this hideous effect. A *society* could, as exemplified in the "two or three gathered together" in Jesus' original terms (surely not as exemplified in Christendom) or as exemplified by Don Juan and Don Genaro.

Chapter 10. *Roof-Brain Chatter*

1. In *The Psychology of Intelligence,* (Littlefield, Adam & Co., 1960, p. 32) Jean Piaget speaks of verbal behavior as ". . . a rough draft of action–which runs the constant risk of being nothing more than a plan . . . [replacing] things by signs and movements by their evocation, and continues to operate by means of these spokesmen." (If I read my old notes correctly, Piaget refers to "roof-brain chatter.")

Interlude:

1. From Sally Carrighar's *Wild Heritage.*
2. From Edmund Carpenter's *Eskimo Realities.*
3. Cassirer, p. 99.
4. The sociological effect of literacy and printing has long been a topic with Marshall McLuhan, Harold A. Innis, and others. See: *The Guttenberg Galaxy* by McLuhan, and *Explorations in Communication* by Carpenter and McLuhan.

Chapter 11. *Double Mindedness*

1. The suggestion was given me that learning to read might influence hemispheric speech separation. The eyes are always moving to the right to

interact with new data in reading. The mind starts anticipating reality as an organization geared from the right. Semantic orientation begins a general swing to "rightness" for consensus security. As Jean Houston points out, physical movements of the body become increasingly locked into set patterns as the child's acculturation extends. (Visual influence over muscular movement is explored by Feldenkreis.)

2. According to Ira Progoff, (p. 151, 152), Carl Jung and Einstein used to lunch together in their young days in Zurich. Jung found Einstein "analytical" and difficult to communicate with concerning "unconscious processes." Einstein, according to Jung, hadn't much "aptitude for the symbolic dimensions of experience."

   On the other hand, Einstein's private papers disclose that dreams and images played important roles in his creative life. I would suggest that our "primary experience" bears much greater similarity than our surface ego-communications indicate.

Chapter 13. *Mind Engineering*

1. *Time* Magazine did a devastating "hatchet job" on Yuri Geller (and others). *Time* selected those events and circumstances thoroughly discrediting Geller. *Time* also grouped such meticulous researchers as Charles Tart with highly suspect and careless showmen, tarring all with the same brush. Guilt by association is hardly objective journalism. Nevertheless, most "nonordinary" phenomena *are* subjective and not amenable to cultural "prediction and control." This has been one

issue of my book. Should Geller-type material become fully acceptable within such channels of the culture as *Time,* we would know that the cultural force would have absorbed, and destroyed, the *Crack*-sign value of such phenomena. When those working in the field of "nonordinary" phenomena stop trying to prove to the *Establishment,* they will make a great leap forward. Anonymity is the direction.

2. Arigo fits in with phenomena with which I am well acquainted, and which is not so very rare. But the sensational approach taken by those who would "publish abroad" the story of Arigo tends to undermine and discredit the open-endedness contained therein. Robert Jeffries, of the University of Bristol, Connecticut, has probably uncovered as "sensational paranormal" material as anyone. He approaches his material with a quiet dignity, however, a reserve that is admirable and lends to his efforts considerable credibility. The same approach is found in Charles Tart, of the University of California at Davis.

Chapter 15. *Reversibility Thinking*

1. Don Juan's *controlled dreaming* has a long tradition, though we are continually left with an incomplete picture of the phenomena. Robert Monroe's strange "astral travel" experiences are no doubt within the same area of mental activity.

   Don Juan's lifestyle, or "Path," contains within it every major feature from all the important traditional disciplines of the world. All these diverse elements are contained within a totally coherent, consistent, and interrelating pattern, lending credit to the authenticity of Carlos's work. Were Don Juan a figment of Carlos's creative imagination, we would nevertheless have to acknowledge Carlos as the principal psychological, spiritual, and literary genius of recent generations. Either way, Don Juan is the most important paradigm since Jesus.

Chapter 16. *Embracing Despair*

1. Academic scoffings and occultic misappropriations concerning Cleve Backster's work must, as usual, be attributed as much to Backster's enthusiasts as to the "close-mindedness" of his detractors. Again we find the loss of balance and indiscriminate acceptancies in "plant consciousness" as in other areas. In spite of nonesense overlaid, Backster's contention fits with the whole picture of life and consciousness.
2. Boone wrote his little volume long before the current explosion of nonordinary interests. Boone's experience fits well with traditions of the American Indian, the Australian Aborigine, don Juan, and others.
3. This beautiful statement of an "extraverted" mystical type experience was sent me by Bodhan Hodiak, of Pittsburgh, Pennsylvania. Since my own childhood contained such experiences, and my own children have reported similar "unity" events in the course of their growing up, I believe this phenomena to be continually trying to break through the rigidities of our semantic fixations.

Bibliography

Boone, J. Allen, *Kinship with All Life*. New York, Harper & Row, 1954.

Brown, J. Spencer. *Laws of Form*. New York, The Julian Press, 1972.

Bruner, Jerome S. *On Knowing*—Essays for the left hand. Cambridge, Belknap Press, 1962.

——. *A Study of Thinking* (with Goodnow and Austin). New York, Science Editions, 1962.

Carpenter, Edmund. *Eskimo Realities*. New York, Holt, Rinehart & Winston, 1973.

Carrighar, Sally. *Wild Heritage*. Boston, Houghton Mifflin, 1965.

Cassirer, Ernst. *Language and Myth*. New York, Harper and Bros., 1946.

Castaneda, Carlos *The Teachings of Don Juan*—A Yaqui way of knowledge. Berkeley, University of California Press, 1968.

——. *A Separate Reality*. New York, Simon and Schuster, 1971.

——. *Journey to Ixtlan.* New York, Simon and Schuster, 1972.

Chang Chung-Yuan. *Creativity and Taoism.* New York, Harper and Row, 1970.

Cherry, Colin. *On Human Communication.* Cambridge, M.I.T. Press, 1951.

de Ropp, Robert. *The Master Game.* New York, Delacorte, 1968.

Fair, Charles M. *The Physical Foundation of the Psyche.* Middletown, Wesleyan U. Press.

Furth, Hans G. *Thinking without Language* – psychological implications of deafness. New York, Free Press, 1966.

Gardner, Martin. *The Ambidextrous Universe*–left, right, and the fall of parity. New York, Basic Books, 1964.

Gregory, R. L. *Eye and Brain* – the psychology of seeing. New York, McGraw-Hill 1966.

Herrigel, Eugen. *Zen in the Art of Archery.* New York, Pantheon, 1953.

Huxley, Aldous. *The Doors of Perception.* New York, Harper and Row, 1954.

Innis, Harold A. *The Bias of Communication.* University of Toronto Press, 1951.

Jensen, Adolf E. *Myth and Cult Among Primitive Peoples.* Chicago, University of Chicago Press, 1963.

Jung, Carl G. *Memories, Dreams, Reflections.* New York, Pantheon, 1963.

Langer, Susanne K. *Mind: an Essay on Human Feeling.* Baltimore, Vol. I, 1970. Johns Hopkins University Press.

Latner, Joel. *The Gestalt Therapy Book.* New York, The Julian Press, 1973.

Lee, Dorothy. "Lineal and Non-lineal Codifications of Reality," from: *Explorations in Communication,* Edmund Carpenter and Marshall McLuhan. Boston Beacon Press, 1960.

Legge, J. *The Texts of Taoism.* New York, the Julian Press 1959.

Lilly, John C. *Programming and Metaprogramming in the Human Biocomputer.* New York, The Julian Press, 1972.

Luce, Gay Gear. *Current Research in Sleep and Dreams.* Public Health Service Publication #1389.

Masters, Robert, and Houston, Jean. *Mind Games.* New York, Viking Press, 1972.

Mathieson, Peter. *Under the Mountain Wall*–two seasons in a stone age culture. New York, Viking Press, 1962.

Melzacks, Ronald. "How Acupuncture Works"–the gate theory of pain. *Psychology Today* Magazine, June 1973.

Monroe, Robert A. *Journeys Out of the Body.* Garden City, Doubleday, 1971.

Myklebust, Helmer R. *The Psychology of Deafness.* New York, Greene and Stratton, 1960.

Neihardt, John C. *Black Elk Speaks.* New York, Pocket Books, 1972.

Ornstein, Robert E. *The Psychology of Consciousness.* W. H. Freeman, 1971.

——. "Right and Left Thinking," *"Psychology Today,* May, 1973.

Owen, A.R.G. *Can We Explain the Poltergeist?* Helix Press, 1964.

Pearce, Joseph Chilton. *The Crack in the Cosmic Egg*. New York, The Julian Press, 1971.

Piaget, Jean. *The Origins of Intelligence in Children.* New York, International Universities Press, 1952.

——. *Play, Dreams, and Imitation in Childhood.* New York, W.W. Norton, 1962.

Pines, Maya. "We are Left Brained or Right Brained" from *The New York Times Magazine,* Sept. 9, 1973.

Polanyi, Michael. *The Study of Man.* Chicago, University of Chicago Press, 1959.

Progoff, Ira. *Jung Synchronicity, and Human Destiny.* New York, The Julian Press, 1973.

Sperry, R. W. "Apparent doubling of consciousness in each hemisphere," *American Psychologist,* Vol 23 # 10, Oct., 1968.

——. "Conscious phenomena as direct emergent properties of the brain. . ." *Psychological Review,* Vol 77 #6, Nov. 1970.

——. "A Molified Concept of Consciousness". *Psychological Review,* Vol. 76, 1969.

Sullivan, Harry Stack. *The Interpersonal Theory of Psychiatry.* New York, W. W. Norton, 1953.

Tart, Charles T. *Altered States of Consciousness.* New York, John Wiley & Sons, 1969.

——. "Physiological correlates of psi cognition." *International Journal of Parapsychology,* 1963 Vol 5, pp. 375-386.

Welch, Holmes. *The Parting of the Way.* Boston, Beacon Press, 1966.

White, Leslie A. *Science of Culture*–a study of man and civilization. New York, Noonday, 1969.

Whitehead, Alfred North. *Science and the Modern World.* Macmillan, 1925.

Wilhelm, Richard, and Jung, Carl G. *The Secret of the Golden Flower*. New York, Harcourt Brace, 1962.

Wolff, Franklin Merrell. *The Philosophy of Consciousness without an object*. New York, The Julian Press, 1973.